Overcoming Worldly Concerns

Fr. Alban Goodier, SJ

Overcoming
Worldly Concerns

SOPHIA INSTITUTE PRESS
Manchester, New Hampshire

Nihil obstat: Edward Myers, *Censor Deputatus*
Imprimatur: Edm. Can. Surmont, *Vicarius Generalis*
Westminster, March 9, 1914

Sophia Institute Press
Box 5284, Manchester, NH 03108
1-800-888-9344

www.SophiaInstitute.com

Sophia Institute Press® is a registered trademark of Sophia Institute.

paperback ISBN 978-1-64413-700-0

ebook ISBN 978-1-64413-701-7

Library of Congress Control Number: 2022932338

First printing

Contents

Overcoming Worldly Concerns

Chapter 1

Your Inner Self Speaks the Truth to You

It is a truism to say that we all live two lives; but it may not be useless to examine what they are and to see something of their relation to each other. There is the life that appears outside, which is seen and judged by others, and which occupies the chief, active part of our being; but there is also the other life, quite distinct from this, which seems to be forever sitting back within ourselves and never appearing, but judging every thought, and word, and action of the other, and mercilessly and infallibly telling us whether it is really good or bad, right or wrong, commendable or the reverse, whatever others may say, or whatever we ourselves may try to think. We may affect to ignore it, but although it accepts the rebuff, it will not easily be ignored. We may call it all manner of names, but its very silence compels us to recognize our abuse to be no more than calumny. We may turn our whole attention to the outside, active life, to that which occupies our time, which brings us in contact with others, and which, we tell ourselves, is all that matters; still the silent gnawing at our hearts, speechless but eloquent, beaten down but ever persevering, lets us know beyond possibility of doubt that we are playing false, that we are not so convinced as we pretend, that we are not so happy with ourselves as our words would signify, that we are turning to what we like, not to what we know to be the best, that we cannot deceive our real selves, although for a time we may deceive others, and even that outer self that we try to think is all that we are. Really, at heart, we are not deceived, and we know it; for to deceive ourselves into thinking that we are deceived is no deception.

Let us look at this fact a little more close at hand. Scarcely anything comes across my path, scarcely anything is seen with my eyes or in any other way is borne in upon my mind, without my being conscious that at once, and almost at the same instant, I look on it from two points of view. I see it, perhaps, to be a thing beautiful in itself, or sweet and attractive to me, or something that will serve my purpose; or, on the other hand, it appears to me as something ugly, repulsive, injurious. But almost at the same moment, behind this first and clear apprehension, there is another onlooker within me, less impetuous but more discriminating, who begins to ask, "Is that thing wholly beautiful, or does it appear so only to me? Is it really attractive, or does it suit my palate only here and now? Is it truly of use, or does it serve my purpose only for the moment? Or, again, is it absolutely ugly, repulsive, injurious, or is this appearance only due to something discordant in myself? Is it more than an external coating, covering a wealth of real beauty, and loveliness, and blessing?"

Nor is it only at the first appearance of an object that this double self speaks. At every step we take, an echo of the footfall is heard within. We tell ourselves that a thing is good or bad; at once the voice's question is whether our judgment is sincere, whether it is not made to serve our purpose, declared good because we wish it so. We choose between one thing and another; the voice, heard only by ourselves, asks whether our choice is just and is not rather the concrete expression of a desire long since entertained. We decide on a certain course of action; sometimes the voice dins in our ears that we are wrong and we know it, sometimes it merely reminds us that we have decided too quickly in a matter too momentous; sometimes, when we have made up our minds to have our way, there is heard no more than a distant wailing that haunts us like the lamentation of a ghost.

It is in vain for us to try to silence this inner voice. It is beyond our reach. We cannot gag it; we cannot shut it out for any length of time. We may argue with it and with ourselves; we may prove to verbal conviction that to listen to it is mawkish, scrupulous, paralyzing to all effort, undermining every action; in our hearts, we know very well that the voice is right when it merely answers, without consenting to argue, that it is not true. We may affect not to hear it, we may affect to pity those who do, or to be interested in the psychological phenomenon they represent; we know that our affectation is that and no more, that our pity has been learned at home, in practice upon ourselves, before it has shown itself abroad. We may proclaim against the tyranny; we may call it superstition; we may stigmatize it as the fruit of generations of priestcraft; we may call it every ugly name we like and treat it with every kind of contempt or condescension; all the time it tells us, and we know it to be true, that in saying all this we are disloyal to ourselves and to mankind, that it is the safeguard of the noblest that is in us, that it is our one guarantee—to ourselves if not to others—that we are men, and living in a manner worthy of our manhood, that to stifle this voice, to use violence against it and throttle it, to be heartless and silently to defy it is to inflict upon ourselves the murder of the best being that is in us.

No matter how we try, no matter how well we may play our part, we shall never succeed in deceiving ourselves altogether; if we did, we would have killed our very human nature. For a time, it is true, it is possible to forget and to ignore without adverting. We may for a season fill our lives with noise, with a whirl of tumult and excitement, with a temporary fascination, but after noise must come silence; excitement must rest to recuperate; every fascination has its awakening; then we return to ourselves, and deception is impossible, except, as we have said, that we may deceive ourselves into thinking that we are deceived. We appeal to our former convictions; we say we have these same convictions still; but with all our convictions, we remain unconvinced. The voice that is unceasing within us is truer to us than we are to ourselves. It bides its time; it renews its wailing; it persists even though we bid it to stop, even though we close up our ears, even though we abuse it, even though we pervert its words, even though before others, by word and action, we give it the lie; it persists, and in spite of all, if we will allow it, it will save us. Not only that, but will make of us the perfect creature that God and nature have both destined us to be.

And this, in our sober moments, when at last we acknowledge ourselves beaten, or when we are at peace and untroubled by any particular fascination, we see without any doubt. We may have reveled in the whirl of what we call life, whether it be the whirl of its joys or of its business or of its interests, but in our hearts, when we are either free or compelled to judge, we know that there is a reality greater than all these. We know that the man whose life is wholly filled with these things misses the chief part of his manhood. He lives their life; he does not live his own. He may claim to be free and to be living according to his own choice; but his freedom is subjected to them, and his choice is made at their dictation. The real man within him is dwarfed in his growth, and it is the knowledge of this, conscious and emphasized with time, however resented and denied, that gradually banishes the laughter from his face and fills his latter days with a void, with a certain sense of self-contempt, with bitterness and failure. He fills the void with indulgence, but the indulgence rings of despair.

To anticipate and prevent this collapse, to guard against this self-deception and its consequences, is the aim and meaning of the spiritual life. The spiritual life is not a mere matter of devotion; not, at all events, of devotion as the word is commonly understood. Devotions in themselves are good, as all else in itself is good; but devotions are as liable to lead to self-deception as every other thing that attracts. The spiritual life goes deeper down; it aims at the making of the man, not on the surface only, but working outward from within. It would have a man first and foremost live according to the voice that in his heart he knows to be truest. It would have him learn to recognize the voice and listen to its teaching. It would have him weigh his judgments by what that voice suggests, and choose as that voice dictates, not as his meaner self demands. It would have him be free, and would make him free, not with that counterfeit freedom that must obey the dictate of indulgence, but with the freedom which can say yes or no at will. It would have him be a man, not of mere flesh and blood, which are entirely slavish and dependent, but of spirit and soul, which are masters of themselves and all the world.

Chapter 2

Rising above the Ways of the World Will Bring You Happiness

In every language there are words that have a sense of staleness about them. As soon as we hear them, we tell ourselves, with a shrug of the shoulders, that we have heard them before, that we know all they mean, that those who use them are old-fashioned people, rather dull, and certainly unoriginal. We even go so far, in proof that these words have been worn threadbare, as to use them in some more flippant sense, giving them a kind of galvanized new life, since their real life is gone. Thus, we will tell our friends, with a touch of self-complacency, that we fear we are a bit of a heathen, or something of a loose fish, or we will use some other sorry title that, we hope, will be equally shocking and gallant.

One of these old-fashioned words is *worldliness*, and another its concomitant, *worldling*; to be called a worldling smacks of the unconventional, independent, generous, large-hearted, and suggests, on the whole, a rather agreeable sort of companion. When a man lays claim to the title, he means us to understand that he knows a thing or two, that he has found experience at first hand, that he has not feared to drink of life at its sources or beneath the surface of the stream, that he sees more in the world, and in men and women, than the common run of mortals have seen, that he has tasted of the tree of knowledge of good and evil and has found the fruit worth the venture. The worldling, so he tells his friends, can forgive all because he knows all. He has a kindly word for every backslider, so long as they slide backward along the way of the world. He pities those who aim at being better, as having no more sense, and as acting out of ignorance; or he twits them for their moonshine ideas; or, if that cannot convert them, he condemns them as prigs, who presume to set themselves above their equals.

And yet there is something behind all this that makes complete deception impossible. The worldling is conscious, while he speaks, that all is not quite as he describes it. At the same time, the onlooker, while he laughs and makes a show of approval, knows very well that there are other things beneath the surface. In other words, to be quite plain spoken, both are well aware that worldliness is a lie—a lie in the heart, that peculiarly loathsome kind of lie that is characteristic of a coward.

The worldling may affect to be a happy man; he may set himself up as more human than his comrades; but he knows in his heart, without a doubt, that he is a traitor to his human nature, and a mean fellow. He knows that he acts against his right convictions, that he crushes them down beneath his heel, and that he sacrifices that within him which might have grown to something great, for a prize that is beneath contempt. If he did not know, it would be different; he would not be called a worldling, simply because his heart could not prove him a craven. The pig that swills in its trough, even the savage that eats and drinks himself stupid: these may not be called worldly, because they know no better; but the man who does know better, yet is content to swill, wallowing in what this world has to offer, be it gold, or rioting, or luxury, or even base ambition, such a man narrows his margin to that of any beast, is a traitor to the manhood that is in him, and when he affects to find in this the fulfillment of his life's desire, that downtrodden manhood still tells him that he lies.

So mean a thing is worldliness, and so mean a creature is a worldling! He determines to be content with his immediate surroundings and is irritated at the suspicion, approaching to a certainty, that there is something better, more worthy of a man's ambitions, in his reach. This he cannot in his heart deny; to do so in word and deed effects little, so he decides to ignore it, to treat it as if it were not, as one might decide to live content in a haunted house by ignoring the ghost that wandered through it. True, it is a cheap sort of victory, but it serves its purpose, for it turns real life into an elaborate make-believe, that gigantic sham of which so much of this life is made up, and which must be what it is, being built upon a lie.

Being that within, the worldling must adapt all that comes within his sphere to fit into the same perspective. He would like to estimate everything—right and truth, as well as coal and provender—by immediate weights and measures, by their present market value, by their conformity with existing regulations. Right is that which is according to the life he has decided to live; truth is truth insofar as it does not contradict his accepted postulate; and he protests, sometimes to bloody persecution, always with relentless hatred, against those who prefer less conventional scales of measurement. Such men he cannot leave alone, for they keep alive a memory that he hopes he might otherwise learn to forget. Or, again, he would have this life stand still; he would gladly settle down here for all eternity; but since that cannot be, he would at least pretend that it is and let the end come unawares.

So is the worldling a coward, for he has not the courage of his convictions; so is he a mean creature, for, not having the courage of his convictions, he must hide his cowardice by mean devices; so is he a liar, for only by a lie can he justify himself, whether to man without, or to that complaining, questioning voice which warns him of his treachery within.

Nor is this only the aspect of the worldling, considered in the light of the spiritual life; if, indeed, a distinction can be made between the spiritual and the real. Whatever he may say in a flippant mood, every man, the more he is a man, the more he scorns to be a worldling; apart from any sense of religion, the very human nature that is in him tells him he has ideals higher than those of the brute. He believes himself endowed with higher powers, made master of the world, for some other end than simply to live a brutish life in a rather more exquisite manner; indeed, here is the essence of that which he understands by *character*. For character stands for what is right; character slashes itself free from the bondage of its surroundings; character puts duty above convenience. Worldliness knows none of these things; when unmasked, it is no more nor less than lack of character.

Still, these two are not strictly antithetical. One is but the denial of the other; it is not its opposite. For character is merely unworldly, and unworldly according to its grade. To discover the opposite, it must be remembered what *worldliness* rightly means. By *worldliness* we mean this-worldliness; and the opposite of this is the worldliness of another world. Otherworldliness introduces other standards, other ideals, and therefore other perspectives; it does not destroy or lessen the value of things of earth; it only puts them in another and more accurate relation. Other-worldliness begins by accepting the dictate of that inner voice which proclaims the more enduring truth, in opposition to the voice that bids us be contented with the present. It recognizes a broader reality than that which appears to the eyes or is enjoyed by our other senses. It accepts the principle that a greater end must absorb a lesser, that a greater end ennobles a lesser, that therefore the greater and deeper life of man must absorb and give meaning to the surface life of his little day, and that he should himself, in his nature of man, be master of all that is included in his manhood.

This is the teaching of all wisdom, pagan or Christian, temporal or spiritual, ethical or religious; in whatever else they differ, they agree in condemning worldliness. To live for this world is to degrade our human nature; to live above this world is alone to live like a man. But to live above this world demands another world in which and for which we may live; and this demand is met, in part by a world of intellect, which some men fashion for themselves, in full only by that real other-world, in which we Christians believe. This is the key to the secret of the saints. Whatever else they were, they were men; eccentric if you like, offensive if you like, fanatical and misguided, but tingling essences of human nature, humanity at its boiling point. This mere unworldliness could never have produced much less life for this world. It was the acceptance, whole-hearted and unflinching, of the inner truth that made them, and the consequent realization of that other world in which they moved. For that world, accordingly, they lived; living for it, they took this life in their stride. Its sweets were only relatively sweet; its barriers were too trifling to hinder them; and while smaller men peep at them to find reasons to condemn, they are staggered by the lives they lived.

Says St. John Chrysostom[1], "Nothing so wears out a man as to be sodden with the love of things earthly."

---

[1] St. John Chrysostom (c. 347-407), Archbishop of Constantinople and Doctor; named Chrysostom, or "Golden Mouth," for his eloquent preaching.

Chapter 3

The Very Fact of God's Existence Gives Meaning to Your Life

If it did not much matter whether man believed in God or not, there can be little doubt that many more would acknowledge their belief in Him than actually do. If men could be allowed to accept God and still live exactly as they pleased, if they could treat Him as a power who belonged to quite a different sphere and had no concern with this world, or as a friendly neighbor or an acquaintance or a distant relation, who looked to his own affairs and left us free to look after ours, then it is not improbable that the proofs and signs of His existence would be received with less questioning and opposition.

Indeed, there is scarcely a man who lays claim to common sense and is not the victim of his own violent mind, who does not acknowledge at least a Supreme Being somewhat of this nature. When the old paganism had outgrown its many gods, and had settled down to a life of self-indulgence, it still accepted the belief in a God who cared little or nothing for mankind; and the modern paganism, impatient of all interference from without, believes in much the same way, and in the same way buries its

God behind a cloud. Is there a priest, with any experience of so-called unbelievers, who has not again and again heard this profession of faith: "I believe in something supreme," to which, however, this corollary has been added or implied: "Who is no concern of mine"?

But it is precisely because an explicit act of faith in God cannot stop at that and be done with, that to many it comes so much against the grain. If we say positively that God is, there follow no end of consequences—consequences by no means congenial to the man who wishes and intends to manage his life according to his own sweet will. So that, rather than commit itself by making this first admission, rather than allow itself to be convicted of falsehood or inconsistency, human nature instinctively prefers to make no admission at all, or to set the question aside and to substitute others in its stead. To make no admission, to assume an attitude of doubt, to say one has not been able finally to decide is the commonest and easiest course; for this a man can do with an abundant show of reason—nay, more, with an abundant show of honesty. He can appeal to a sense of duty and declare that his life is too full to allow him time and opportunity to arrive at a final conclusion about God; he can be diffident and humble and say that he is too dull of understanding, too lacking in technical training, to attempt so intricate a problem; he can claim to be broadminded and unbiased, and therefore, to avoid overemphasis, to appreciate too keenly the gropings of other minds to be sternly dogmatic himself; or he may be studious, learned, a hard reader, and maintain that the doubts of greater minds than his own justify his own hesitation, while the almost infinite succession of blunders on this point in past ages justifies his disbelief in a definite solution, justifies even his leaving the question altogether alone. In countless ways, when driven to speak, the man who says he doubts the fact of God can make out a good defense; yet more often he prefers to say nothing, but to let the question die unanswered.

For, as a matter of fact, men know that there are other proofs of truth than those of argument; upon argument alone men accept very little; they do not even arrange their lives by it. In their hearts they know that to deny God outright, no matter with what show of reason, is merely foolish. Where the most a man can claim is ignorance, it is foolish positively to deny; there is no greater folly than to argue from one's ignorance of a thing to the conclusion that the thing is not.

But common sense does not stop there; not only does it prove downright atheism to be no more than arrogant folly, but it also compels other admissions. The man who confesses his own ignorance implicitly confesses that others may know better than he. The man who acknowledges that he never gives the matter a thought must also acknowledge that others who do may probably have reached conclusions that he has not. Common sense makes him suspect that, in that case, they are more likely to be right; while his common instincts instantly drive him to act on the assumption that God is, and that he matters to God, and that God matters to him. At many a sudden turn in his life, his very human nature betrays him into acting as one who believes, even while he affects not to care, and the man who did not he would despise as one who had debased his manhood.

This is no place for theological discussion. We have no need here even to summarize the proofs of the fact of God. We are addressing those who know, although, in any case, to very few people indeed does the fact of God depend upon proof, as the word is commonly understood. To most it is a "certainty greater than reason." On that account are men and women willing to die for it, who would not die for the conclusion of a syllogism. We have only to sit back and watch human nature, at all times, under all circumstances, in every condition of life, either writhing and resisting under the intolerable burden of God, or gladly accepting Him and finding Him a yoke that is sweet and a burden that is light[2], we shall then realize how great a confession of the fact of God is human life itself. Man is too terribly conscious of God for God not to be or not to matter. However independent and self-governed he may be, he cannot leave God alone. He can scarcely act without the wonder coming to him as to what that Other One may think; he cannot follow his own likes or dislikes as he wills, simply because Something Else says he must not. Whichever way he turns, God confronts him; even if he looks into his heart, he finds Him there. If he leaves God aside, he knows he does so by convention, not by conviction. So it has always been; this, at least, evolution has not mended, and so he knows it always will be, whatever evolution may say.

In face of this fact, as has just been said, man is driven to one of two attitudes. "He who is not with me is against me."[3] He may indeed claim a third position; he may claim to follow a middle course; but to pass God by is to refuse Him. Either man finds God an intolerable burden, and does all he can to shake Him off, or he believes that the burden is a blessing, that truth, rightly understood, cannot be tyrannical or cruel, accepts God, and has a happy heart as his reward. One man chooses what he sees, blinds himself to what he does not, makes for himself a working creed, a working code of moral action, a conventional understanding of life, based on the assumption that this world is all there is, and that no other concerns him. By signing that

[2] See Matt. 11:30.
[3] Matt. 12:30.

convention, by abiding to that code, he succeeds in hemming himself within a charmed circle, which may serve him as long as he lives, and which may hide from him for that length of time the weird visions that haunt the space without. But his security he knows to be unsound; his peace of mind is unreal, for he has not known the things that were to his peace; he cries for it and there is none. Another knows of no such charmed circle. He does not believe that life is made truer by any confinement of horizon. He is open to the truth from whatever side it may come; he believes life is deeper than convention, that this world is not all existence; he has more reverence for right and wrong than to think that it can be fixed, or sanctioned, or regulated, by any human code. As a vessel is most itself when out on the ocean rather than when cooped up in the stocks, so is the life of man most real when it lies and is tossed on the infinite ocean of God.

Such a man lets this life dictate to him the fact of God, and its evidence is overwhelming. He lets the fact of God be to him the key to life, and it solves every mystery; and, accepting the key, he accepts the consequences of its possession. If God is, God counts. If God counts, He counts for more than man, for more than all creation put together. If He counts for more than all this, His mind must be considered, His will must be fulfilled, and the finding of that mind, the fulfillment of that will somehow explains the riddle of the world. And if it explains that riddle, it is also the secret of the happiness of life. Human nature may, at times, resent; it may long to shake off its harness, but it knows very well—and too often experience has confirmed the knowledge—that to live without God leads to death and to lasting fetters, even when the death of life has no more than cast its shadow over it. "The fear of the Lord is honor, and glory, and gladness, and a crown of joy. The fear of the Lord shall delight the heart, and shall give joy, and gladness, and length of days. With him that feareth the Lord it shall be well in the latter end, and in the day of his death he shall be blessed. The love of God is honorable wisdom."[4]

---

[4] Ecclus. 1:11-14 (RSV = Sir. 1:11-14).

Chapter 4

God Calls You to Take Responsibility
for Your Choices

No men really, few men even in appearance, care to be convicted
of deliberate wrongdoing. Even in his own eyes, before the tribu-
nal of his own conscience, a man prefers to be found not guilty.
Our most deliberate and barefaced misdeeds we would gladly
clothe in at least a semblance of good. To secure this, we make
smooth excuses that we know will not bear examination. We frame
convenient definitions of right and wrong to suit our particular
case. We put the blame on others, or on our circumstances, or
on our want of knowledge, for things entirely our own fault. We
plead ignorance, weakness, or inexperience. In a hundred ways
we wriggle and writhe about to escape the pointing of the finger
at us. This is true, even when the misdeed is known to ourselves
alone. We argue with ourselves; we pretend to convince ourselves
that we are not guilty, that we have even done a virtuous act, that
if we really take all the facts into consideration, the evidence is
entirely in our favor.

It is even truer in regard to others. Even if we cannot quite convince ourselves of our simple innocence, or, if we prefer it to be so

called, of our straightforward manliness, others shall not be given the chance to doubt; others shall not be suffered to question our singleness of view. They shall see how we do not even suspect the possibility of an adverse judgment. They shall be overwhelmed by our utter certainty and genuineness. They shall be given no room for a reflection that shall redound to our discredit.

But if this is true in regard both to ourselves and to others, still more is it true in regard to God. If God is, we wish to stand well with Him; since God is, not to stand well with Him is the greatest evil. If God is, His will must be considered; since God is, to go against that will is to do great wrong, for which, so common sense dictates, somewhere, somehow, I must pay the penalty. And yet I cannot deceive God. Others I can deceive, myself I can think I deceive, but God there is no deceiving. Before Him I cannot play a part. I cannot even conjure up excuses; I cannot frame a definition, an argument, or a brief for the defense that shall save my face if I really am guilty. How, then, can I escape?

There is but one way. If I cannot deceive God, I can at least deceive myself in regard to God. I can throw doubt on the fact of God; I can eliminate God from my horizon. By so doing, I can hope that my deeds may be judged without any reference to Him. Judged on another scale—the scale, let us say, of human standards, or the scale of convention, or the scale of expediency, all of which agree to look at life with one eye covered—they may be easily condoned or justified. "This satisfaction or that," so I argue with myself, "my nature goads me on to seek. But the law of God says I may not have it. Now, if that law did not exist, what would remain to thwart me? If I could free myself from its authority, if I could justify myself in ignoring it, I might have my way. The will is father to the thought. I will sift the authority of this law until I find questions that cannot be answered; I will examine the evidence of its Maker until I formulate problems that have no solution. Or I will justify myself on my own side, by discovering my own ignorance, by proclaiming my perplexity, so that I may doubt His being, or His sovereignty, or His interest in men, or something else about Him, it matters little what, so long as it shakes His authority over me. For doubting Him, I am further justified in doubting the law He is reputed to have made; and a doubtful law binds no one."

For how much unbelief, as has been said elsewhere, does this line of argument account! How much unbelief depends, not on doubt of doctrine, not on actual ignorance, but on moral restlessness and resentment of restraint! How many unbelievers have first sinned, have first thrown away their innocence, and then have fled to unbelief, or have been goaded to it, as the one escape from the lashing of their conscience! While they were sinless, they saw clearly enough, and understood, and could not doubt. Having sinned, they are blind, they are glad they cannot see, they permit themselves to come to no conclusion, but bury, so they fondly hope, one grim fact beneath the toppled-down ruins of another. But it will not be buried; it will not even be slain. The serpent has been scotched, no more, and that only for a time. Soon it wriggles itself loose and crawls to the summit of the ruins, and raises its hissing head, and man discovers that in spite of all his efforts, and of all his sacrifice of truth, "his sin is always before him."[5]

Nor does it avail him any better to invent convenient subterfuges, however plausible and humane they may appear. He may claim that he does no harm to anyone and that therefore no one can blame him; he knows that this is not the whole matter, that sin includes more than his relations to his fellowmen, that a man

[5] See Ps. 50:5 (RSV = Ps. 51:3).

can be a cad or a beast independently of any but himself, that at times injury to others may even become an act of noblest virtue.

Or he may rise a little higher and declare that he does no more than live according to the dictates of humanity. He is still conscious that the dictates of humanity cover but a very small area of life; that his moral horizon reaches far beyond the narrowed realm of human authority; that right and wrong are independent of creation itself; that, far from being the dictate of humanity, they rather are its dictators.

Or he may go to the opposite extreme. He may ask, "What is truth?" and decline to wait for an answer.[6] He may say that, after all, right and wrong in themselves are very doubtful; that they differ in different people; that they depend very much on individual point of view; that they matter very little in practice; that right more often comes to grief where evil prospers; that, in this workaday world, we must take things as we find them, and not be too fastidious; that, in the words of Scripture, "he has sinned, and what evil has befallen him?"; that the important thing is not to be disgraced, but, if that secured, little matters.

Or, lastly, he may give up the struggle. He may declare that to resist is impossible; for the serpent, while it hisses, also fascinates. But to yield is a species of despair, and despair is its own condemnation, as well as its own tormentor. It is the nearest point to Hell that man can reach in this life. This plea, then, stands convicted out of its own words; no man is compelled to offend God; to sin perforce is a contradiction in terms. It avails nothing to say that sin is inevitable; that it is but the necessary consequence of human nature; that it is dictated by nature, enforced by nature, and that man but the slave of himself. It is no defense to claim that every man

6   See John 18:38.

24

at times is abnormal; that sin is but temporary insanity, to which every man is occasionally liable, and that the common sentence passed on the suicide should be passed on every sinner who has committed sin. It profits little to become defiant, to maintain that sin is not so much the doom of man as, rather, his characteristic feature; that man is then most a man when he sins; that great men are mostly great sinners, while those who have never sinned are puny, inexperienced, undeveloped.

Such, however veiled, is the language of despair, and despair that defends itself knows that it lies. If a man must sin, then he never sins; for sin is a free man's act. And yet it is also a slavery, the slavery of him that has found his belly's satisfaction in the husks the swine eat;[7] no wonder, then, that it lies to hide its shame. But the shame has little to do with men, above all with men who wallow in the same trough. It points to another onlooker. If "my sin is always before me," it is because He is always before me, from whom I cannot hide. Whichever way man turns, he comes back to the same point: sin is sin, because God is God, and neither can be evaded.

And why should they? To shirk the truth is the action of a coward and must meet with a coward's reward; to accept it, with all its consequences, is alone worthy of a man. Accepting God, man must accept sin; true, but accepting God and sin, he also gives a nobler and a greater significance to all morality. Life is then no longer a mere course of law-girt duty, it is a course of heroic love. It is no longer the grudged service of a slave of nature; it is the willing service of a son. Being free, it is responsible; being responsible, it has the power to do wrong; but on that very account, and on that alone, it is the glorious thing it is.

7 See Luke 15:16.

Let a man accept that responsibility as a man, keep it as a man, and he will receive a man's reward; let him reject it, let him serve himself, and he will meet with his desert, which is the wreck of his manhood. This is sin, and this is sin's wages. As St. Paul says, "The wages of sin is death."[8]

[8] Rom. 6:23.

Chapter 5

Even Your Forgiven Sins Leave
Sorrow in Your Soul

I once did a great injury to a very dear friend. Something he had
done had tried me; something he had said had roused me. I was
bitter at the moment, reckless of consequences. At the same time,
I knew within my heart that his friendship would bear the strain.
I let myself go; I spoke the stinging word, did the wounding deed,
turned on my heel, and slighted him. He took the insult and said
nothing. He was older, greater, than I and could afford to forgo an
apology. When we met again, it was as if nothing cruel had been
done. Since then, we have gone on as before; our friendship has
never diminished.

But I know him too well to suppose that the memory of that
day can ever fade from his mind. I know he has forgiven; in practical life, he has forgotten; but the wound cannot be recalled, and
the scar must always remain. I have never apologized; his manner
has shown me clearly enough that to do so in any form of words
would only be to hurt him the more.

Yet could I forget? The older we grow together, the more I
understand his delicate sympathy of heart, the more I realize what

it is that I have done. It is a lasting shame to me, a lasting agony, which only increases with time. He has forgiven; all the more is it impossible for me to forgive myself. He has forgotten, at least so far as not to let it come between us; all the more can I not forget, but must be drawn the more to him on its account. Although all is past and done with, the sorrow abides; although love has increased, the pain is always there; although friendship has restored me to equality, the craving is greater now than it ever was before to make atonement and to show him that I am true.

I know now of what I am capable; I know now how much his friendship can be trusted; and the fact that we both love each other the more because of what has happened only makes me remember without ceasing the injury that I once did to him. If he were to die, my sorrow would not cease; it is part of the friendship that exists between us, and with that friendship would overleap the grave. My efforts at atonement would not diminish; rather, they would grow. For if death is what I take it to be, I can show him better after death than I ever can show him now the longing that I have in my heart.

If this is true of a friend among men, what shall I say of the Friend of friends? "My sin is always before me." I have done Him an injustice. I have resented the strain of His friendship, sacrificed Him in the face of a trying circumstance, exchanged Him for others whom I had neither the courage nor the character to despise. He has taken the insult and has said nothing; it was not His dignity that was lowered, but mine that was annihilated, by the condescension. He has forgiven, and has told me so, giving me His word as guarantee. He has said that, so far as He is concerned, the past shall be as if it had never happened.

But am I on that account freed from the burden of consciousness of shame? The fact of the insult still remains; the fact of the wound and the scar that marks its place still stands. If I ever forgot that, the agony I have caused, the creature in me that could sink so low, I would be a presuming, arrogant knave. To make atonement is well-nigh useless. He needs no such thing. All the more can I never forget—no, not even though He has died, and has risen, and is in His glory. That does not alter me; it does not alter my action; it only brings home to me the more who it is whom I have offended, what it is that I have done.

This is abiding sorrow, that everlasting element of true contrition. It is consistent with great joy of heart, for it is the outcome of perfect forgiveness. It is consistent with a burning love; indeed, it is its necessary companion. Nonetheless is it an agony; otherwise it would not be sorrow. "Lord, that I had never offended Thee!" Rightly understood, this is a strong heart's cry, and its note is combined of sorrow and gladness, of contrition and love, of the certainty of hope that has routed despair.

Chapter 6

Living an Innocent Life Will Ennoble
You and Bring You Great Rewards

If men are not agreed about the meaning and content of sin,
they are at least agreed about its opposite. If they dispute about
the mystery of evil, if they quarrel with themselves and with one
another concerning wrongdoing and its cause, if they seek to elude
its shame, if they make light of it, or excuse it, or deny it, at least
they are complacent when they are found not guilty. They are
unanimous in agreeing that innocence, I mean the real thing,
has only one interpretation, and that it is altogether beautiful,
admirable, lovable.

It is true that there are those who at times affect another manner. They talk of the necessity of gaining experience; they say
that a man must not be a prig, or maudlin, or sentimental; they
confound innocence with ignorance, simplicity with stupidity,
and grow restless with any attempt at its excessive preservation.
But when they talk like this, they need not be taken too seriously.
It is the outside manner only; it is not the language of the heart.

A man may say that sin is a necessity; yet, if he is a man at all,
and not one of those peculiar, drifting creatures that seem almost

to have squandered away their manhood, he will pay a great price so that his sons and daughters may be guarded from it. He may condone it to shield himself; he would be sorry to see the same defense urged by his wife or children. In his own soul, he may be content to endure its tyranny; but a ruined son, a sinful daughter, is shame that breaks the heart; a sinless son, a spotless daughter, whatever else may or may not be said of either, is the glory of a parent's gray hairs.

So let us say no more of these misunderstandings, which no man who is a man would have us take too much in earnest. For, indeed, what is there in the world more beautiful than innocence? It is the fascination of a child, which is innocent and cannot help it; it is more fascinating still in an understanding girl or boy; in a grown-up man or woman, it is a pearl beyond all price. Men recognize it when they meet it, they hardly know how, and look back at it when it has passed them. Women know it by a kind of instinct, as if its possession were the object of their lives. The world itself, blind and soiled and sodden as it is, knows innocence when it finds it, and either bows before it and suffers it to pass by unscathed or else, if in its devilish mood, lays itself out to despoil it; in either case, it sets up its external signs as the ideals and models for a man to cultivate. The open eye that has no furtive glances, the ringing laugh that has no hollowness, the responsive word that has no restrictions, the face that is all frank, the hand that is all free, the heart that has no hiding places: these are some of the witnesses of innocence, telling, when they are quite true, more eloquently than words can tell, the inward beauty and lovableness of this human nature that is ours.

Nor is innocence only a thing beautiful, a delicate treasure to be kept safe from harm. It is also a thing secure and strong. Innocence will walk through fire and will not burn; it will live amid refuse and will not be stained; it will venture where greater so-called knowledge, greater so-called experience, would not wisely dare, and will come away unscathed. It is its own defense; it believes, because it is true, and is believed in return; it trusts, because it has not in itself the greatest source of doubt, and is trusted. It shows in itself human nature at its best and receives in return the best and the worst of human nature.

When, again, a noble deed is to be done, innocence is best capable of doing it. In the face of death, nothing is so fearless as the innocent hand and the heart that is clean. In the grip of physical torture, under the weight of heavy trial, at times when endurance is taxed to the extreme, there is none that blanches less than the nature that is innocent. Or when action is called for, if one is bidden to do anything, great or small, for God or for man, to drag a poor soul out of the mire, to lift up one's fellowmen from their dead selves to higher things, to teach or to preach, to instruct or to counsel, to serve or to command, innocence will go where guilt may not venture. Innocence will shy at no shadow where guilt will conjure up monsters. Innocence will selflessly act and carry through where guilt will hang its head in confusion. While guilt will be content with a partial gain, innocence will bear all before it. Give me the most loathsome of slum work to be done; give me an innocent and a guilty soul with which to do it; I know which I will choose. Give me children, old or young, to be influenced; I know which will succeed. Give me an honor to be maintained, even a nation to be defended; I know which will be the better champion.

Innocence is straight; innocence is single-minded; innocence is unselfish. It knows no subterfuges; it is generous; it is considerate; it is true. It can be relied upon at times and in places where all else trembles and totters. No wonder men who understand bow down before it in compelled reverence. No wonder they love it; no wonder they long to possess it, if not in themselves, at least in another that they can call their own. When they see its owner robbed and despoiled, no wonder their gorge rises in indignation. This, the fact that at least he knows and is drawn by the fascination of innocence, is the truest part of man, the truest and the best—the part that lets us understand why it is that, in spite of his meanness and infidelity, he is still beloved of God, and an object of keen interest to God's angels.

Yes, to be innocent is worthwhile, to be free from stain of any sort, even, if it must be, at the cost of a little worldly gain, a little worldly knowledge, a little worldly honor, a little worldly satisfaction. Gain cannot affect what I am; knowledge is at best an accretion to my self; honor is seldom the whole truth; satisfaction comes and goes like a dream; but innocence is that which I am, more intimately than the marrow of my bones, as the transparency of glass is the very glass itself. Men honor great deeds done, but it is not the deed so much as its doer that they mean to extol, and it is only by the deed that they know him. Truth can reach farther down; it honors a little child who can do no great deeds, who can do nothing, but yet offers in itself the perfection of a human being. It honors as "our fallen nature's solitary boast" a woman unknown and unnoticed by her own; and because she is surpassingly the greatest of her race, it knows her to be surpassingly innocent. It honors every type of mankind, the blind and the lame, the poor rich and the rich poor, the powerful and the helpless, that has been born, and lived its life, and done everything or seemingly nothing, but has kept itself throughout scatheless, unspotted. And it is wholly right. For what a man does is of value only insofar as it tells us what he is; if he is true—which is the same as saying if he is innocent—he is deserving of all honor, whether he reveals it or not.

When I come to die, and the tale of my life is told, I may or may not be called to account for what I have done or not done. That depends not wholly upon myself. It depends upon the choice of God; it depends upon accidental powers, a few brains more or less, nerve, courage, gifts that God can give or not; it depends still more upon merely accidental circumstances. But whether I am called to account for that or not, it will matter more to me, and it will matter more to God, that I give Him when He asks for it a heart that is true and innocent. God can receive deeds from hands other than mine, and He does not ask them from all. My faithful self is mine and mine only to give Him, and that, whatever else, He will ask for. If I can give Him that, it will be proof enough of a life that has not been lived in vain; proof that He has been with me through it all, and that I shall be with Him through eternity.

Chapter 7

The Saints Prove That You Can
Overcome Weakness and Temptation

It is a strange thing how little we Catholics, who make so much of devotion to the saints, really understand of the secret of sanctity. We read the lives of saints, and we are filled with reverence and admiration. We see their statues in our churches, and we honor them as we might honor some great man who is otherwise no concern of ours. We look at their figures in our stained-glass windows, and we are induced to fancy them to have been different creatures altogether from us; not men and women of living flesh and blood, as we are, but some kind of privileged being, some kind of angel in human form, sent to earth to win our esteem, it may be, but scarcely one of us, scarcely near enough to us to be seriously taken as our friends.

And yet, when we come to understand them better, how very like our own we find their lives to have been: the same kind of trials and temptations, the same sense of failure and shortcoming, the same unceasing disappointments. They, too, knew all the weakness of human nature, and they knew it as much from their own experience of themselves as from what they saw around them. "You do not the things that you would," says St. Paul, writing a word of pity and encouragement to his children in Galatia;[9] but of himself he says no less spontaneously, "I do not that good which I will; but the evil which I hate, that I do." Again, in another place he says, bearing witness to the sense of his great weakness: "I see another law in my members, fighting against the law of my mind, and captivating me in the law of sin that is in my members. Unhappy man that I am, who shall deliver me from the body of this death?"[10]

What a tale all these words tell us of a man who, with all his chosen sanctity, had first-hand knowledge of temptation! And the same may be said of all the saints. All of them who have left any record of their lives in writing tell us how they realized their own great weakness and how they feared for themselves in the face of their temptations.

"Life spends itself in sorrowing, but, indeed, there is no amendment." So writes the great St. Augustine,[11] a man who in his early life had drunk deep of the cup of sin, who had found it so hard to recover, and who to the end of his days felt the consequences of his early misdeeds press hard upon him.

Every morning of his life, we are told, the great St. Philip Neri,[12] that most happy because innocent of saints, added this to his daily prayer: " Have a care of me, O Lord, or I shall certainly betray Thee today."

St. Teresa,[13] who stands so high because of her intimate union with God in prayer, confesses that for seventeen years she was so

---

[9] Gal. 5:17.

[10] Rom. 7:19, 23-24.

[11] St. Augustine (354-430), Bishop of Hippo.

[12] St. Philip Neri (1515-1595), Italian priest who founded of the Congregation of the Oratory.

[13] St. Teresa of Avila (1515-1582), Carmelite nun and mystic who reformed her order.

beset with every temptation that she could scarcely hope to be able to persevere.

St. Alphonsus Liguori,[14] who has written about sin and its nature as has no other Doctor in the Church, was to the end of his days so overcome with scruples and temptations as to be almost persuaded that God had foredoomed him to Hell.

No, in this, at least, the saints were more like us than we imagine, more like us than the written lives sometimes let us see. For the written lives tend to dwell on the golden harvest; they do not always tell us either of the seed-ground or of its tilling. There is no royal road to Heaven, not even for the innocent saints of God. "Man's life on earth is a warfare," says Holy Scripture;[15] it does not say that the saints are excepted. Everyone, whether saint or sinner, whether innocent or guilty, whether priest, religious, or layman, has his particular battle to fight, his particular temptation to conquer, and in that fight, in that conquest, lies precisely the secret of his sanctity. Men and women have worked miracles before today and in the end have been found wanting. Men and women have been raised to great heights of contemplation and prayer and at the last have failed. Men and women have apparently lived lives and died deaths of peace and security, and yet the Just Judge has been compelled to pronounce on them the sentence "Amen, I say to you, I know you not."[16] But no man and no woman yet has fought on against crushing trial and temptation and has failed to win a crown of glory; has stood up and gone onward in spite of past misdeeds and has not been received into the company of the

---

[14] St. Alphonsus Liguori (1696-1787), bishop, Doctor, writer, and founder of the Redemptorists.

[15] See Job 7:1.

[16] Matt. 25:12.

saints. This it is that makes the basis of sanctity, this never giving in, this constant resisting, this refusing to accept the dead level of our own failures. The rest is the structure that is built upon it.

So very human a thing is sanctity, so very ordinary. When the apostle addresses his disciples as those "called to be saints,"[17] he makes no selection; he does not seem to think that he is asking something quite extraordinary. It does not demand special notice; it does not require that a man should live any other life than that which he is living. In every rank of life, under every condition, true sanctity has been and yet can be found. St. Onesimus was a slave; St. Genevieve was a simple shepherdess; St. Isidore was a country farmer; Marie Lataste was a servant girl, St. Benedict Joseph Labre was a common tramp.[18]

And yet we tell ourselves that this can mean nothing for us. In theory it may be very well; in practice it is not possible. We must earn our daily bread; we must endure our circumstances. We are crushed beneath temptations that are inconsistent with sanctity. My own household is against it—a wild and reckless son or brother, a careless, irreligious father or mother, a systematic persecution that is roused to madness by the very shadow of a holy deed. St. Stanislaus[19] was the most innocent of saints, yet for years he lived with, and was in everything subject to, a restless, selfish brother,

---

[17] Rom. 1:7.

[18] St. Onesimus (d. c. 90), freed slave and martyr mentioned in St. Paul's letter to Philemon; St. Genevieve (422-512), patroness of Paris; St. Isidore (d. 1130), Spanish farm worker and example of Christian perfection; Marie Lataste (1822-1847), holy religious of the Society of the Sacred Heart who had a great devotion to the Eucharist; St. Benedict Joseph Labre (1748-1883), pilgrim and mendicant saint.

[19] St. Stanislaus (1031-1079), Bishop of Crackow.

who would kick the poor child to the ground and trample him beneath his feet, because he would not join in his nightly revelry. Is our lot worse than that?

St. Elizabeth[20] was a great saint, although she was turned out of house and home by her brother-in-law to starve with her children in the street, while he sat drinking in his palace. Is it worse for us than that?

And if we speak of our temptations, which one of us will dare to say that we have one particle of the trials, interior and exterior, that some of the saints have been compelled to endure? Nay, more than that—to go no farther than our own immediate surroundings, if we had but the sight of the angels, perhaps if we had but the knowledge of some confessor, if we could but see the battles, far greater than our own, that many around us are fighting, and fighting with success, although they may not know it, we would be shamed into silence when we would complain, and into greater bravery in action.

"Why cannot I do what these and those have done?" This is a question that has turned two sinners into two of the greatest saints in the Church. Before St. Augustine and St. Ignatius of Loyola[21] put it to themselves, no one would have suspected they were the material of which saints are made; and even if they were, no one would have thought that they would have paid the price. What it cost the first we know, at least in part, for he has told us himself, and his story is of the kind that is understood by every human heart.[22] What it cost the second we do not know; but if

---

[20] St. Elizabeth of Hungary (1207-1231), daughter of King Andreas II of Hungary, niece of St. Hedwig, and widow who became a third order Franciscan.

[21] St. Ignatius of Loyola (1491-1556), founder of the Jesuit Order.

[22] See St. Augustine, Confessions.

any master "knew what was in man," he did, and he learned it from his experience of himself.

Indeed, that is the value of it all. The more difficult our particular trial, the greater our particular temptation, so much the more shall we know when our turn comes for action, so much the deeper shall we see into the hearts and lives of others.

Most of us have courage for other things that are hard; if we would only have a little courage for this! If, when temptation is pressing most upon us, we would only not turn cowards and give up! If we would only keep always in mind the words of St. Paul: "God is faithful, who will not suffer you to be tempted beyond that which you can endure, but with the trial will also give the means to overcome it."[23] It is just the little more that we want; it is just because we fail to give the little more, to hold out a very little longer, that all the rest comes to grief. It is just that little more that makes the difference between us and the saints; that little more of spiritual character, not less of trouble and temptation.

[23] 1 Cor. 10:13.

Chapter 8

Christ Has Overcome Death

If there are many platitudes written in the effort to explain life, there
are many more written about death. Indeed, it would seem that there
is nothing that can be written about it that must not in the end be
resolved into one or two obvious remarks. There is nothing new to
be said. We are no wiser now on this point than was the first man
who had to face it; when the last man comes to die, he will know
no more about it than we. Philosophers have analyzed it and have
ended where they began. Poets have attempted to sing of it, and they
have sung nothing more striking than " Death once dead, there's
no more dying then"[24] – surely an obvious truism enough. Spiritual
writers and preachers have discussed it more, perhaps, than they
have discussed any other subject; yet, however impressive they may
have been, all they have had to say has been summed up in some
such statement as that death is certain; that the time and manner
of death are uncertain; that a man dies only once; that death is the
end of this life and of all that is in it, and so forth.

It is true, we can cover these dry bones with fancies of our
own. We can guess at death and imagine what it will be like. We

[24] William Shakespeare, Sonnet 146.

43

can do the very opposite and leave it solemnly alone. Still, the platitudes remain, severely cold and bony, neither to be hidden beneath the trappings of a silken dress, nor to be kept out of the way in a cupboard.

And this is precisely the crux of the whole matter; these platitudes will not be silenced. At other obvious remarks we may yawn in weariness, or we may laugh them out of countenance. If we laugh at these, the grinning skull does not blush for shame; its hollow sockets do not show any indignation, the rows of teeth grin nonetheless. If we yawn, the bones only rattle and awaken us. To be irritated with them, to question their truth, is mere foolishness; from the fact of death, we have not even the escape that we had from the fact of God or the fact of sin. We cannot deny that we shall die, that we shall one day cease to count upon this earth, and all the rest.

Even when we shrug our shoulders and pretend to have no care or fear of the specter, we dread all the time that the cold, clammy finger bones may at any moment be around our neck, perhaps all the sooner because we have turned our back upon it. We may defy it and say that death is nothing to be feared, that it is nothing but an everlasting sleep; it does but echo, and they are ears of a wise man that catch the words: "To sleep, perchance to dream." We may declare that death brings only dissolution; it answers, "What of the soul?" We may say we will be men and will be content to take our chance; it asks, are we sure whether this is manliness or cowardice, it hints that this refusal to face the fact may itself be our condemnation. We may mount our horse and ride away, galloping in a wild career that we may forget it; we turn our head and find that it has gotten up behind us, biding its time until we choose to give it our attention, or until it can claim us for its own.

So whichever way we turn, whatever we may say or do, we are haunted by the endless platitude. "Everything," we read in a daily paper this morning, "can be escaped except death." There was not much news in that, yet more than one reader will have dwelt upon it. The certainty is there, and everyone must face it. The only question is: How may it best be faced? Not many ways are possible.

There is the way of despair; the acknowledgment that death is the one great curse and evil in this world, and on every account and by every means to be avoided and deferred. Along such a road, death is indeed a weird specter; the lives of those who go along that road are indeed haunted lives, very nightmares in which the poor dreamer flies on without ceasing, knowing that in the end he must be overtaken. Of this we need say nothing; common as it is, it is not the attitude of a man, but of a craven.

Then there is the way of ignoring. We hate unpleasant facts; if we cannot escape them, we ignore them; any fallacy suffices to justify our leaving them alone. Whatever may be in store, men tell themselves, at all events here and now life spreads out before them. Death may be tomorrow; today we are alive. Let us, then, eat and drink today; tomorrow shall look to itself. So it is assumed that death will always be tomorrow, not today, and life is lived on that assumption. When at last tomorrow becomes today, it is accepted as an accident that has taken us unawares.

Or, again, there is the attitude of bravado. We can face it, and defy it, and fight it, and be beaten by it, assume that we have met it like men and soldiers, and trust that this will atone for all the rest. This, too, is very bitter; it is close akin to despair.

But there is another attitude. There is the attitude that has been taken up by man from the beginning—the attitude that the world itself accepts as alone consistent with the present life. Man in his heart does not think he is made to be annihilated; to come to the belief that he is, even to the profession of it, whatever he may really believe, demands a forcing of intellect and will that nature itself can scarcely stand. The very fear that haunts a man when he ignores the solemn fact is alone telling evidence against him. He knows that death is the end, but he also thinks it is a beginning. He knows that the present life is good, but he also feels sure that if he dies aright, that which follows will be better. If he dies aright, that is the whole matter. Whether he believes or whether he affects the opposite, he knows it is vital that the verdict should be found in his favor. He will insist that he has lived up to his lights; he will have us reckon only the good done; he has a fellow feeling for those who are already dead and hopes that if he treats them with condoning, so he will be treated in his turn. So he says So-and-so was a good man, taken altogether; or, at all events, that he served his country well; or that he was a good friend; or that he prospered and helped others to prosper; and for the rest it is better left alone.

We do not blame him. "Of the dead let us only speak well" is a good proverb. But it has reference to this side of the grave alone. On the other side, there must be the whole thing or nothing—and there is not nothing.

Then why not face the facts as they are? Whatever men may see about me or may say, whatever outward show I may make, that will remain, and may indeed suffice, on this side of the door. But it is not what appears; it is what I *am* that will pass through—the good in me, the bad, and the indifferent. And when I accept this and make it a factor in my life, at once it alters my perspective. It alters my ideas of right and wrong. It alters my observance of the same. The fact of life-in-death acts at once as a stimulus and a warning, where nothing else will avail. Indeed, if it were not for the fear of the life beyond, the life on this side would soon bring about its own corruption.

And if that is so, or even if it is a half-truth, then death, and the thought of death, cannot be the specter that men make it. Dark as are the wings of the angel of death, they are tipped with gold, lit from the sun that shines beyond, which for the moment he hides from us. And to look death in the face is worthwhile; it is the only manliness. Not as the ancient pagan, who would drink his hemlock or open his vein at command, and calmly, stoically, await the issue; not even as the modern pagan who can boast, but with a strange metallic ring in his laughter, that he will "go to his death like a soldier," as to a doom he cannot avoid; but as those who have kept their eyes toward the light and have so found joy in their sacrifice.

"It is appointed unto men once to die,"[25] and He who has appointed it can do only good; He alone can raise the dead to life. And here at last we have come to a statement about death that is not an obvious platitude. He who has made the dry bones can also make the dry bones live. He can clothe them again with sinews and flesh and skin, can breathe into them the spirit, and make them "stand upon their feet, an exceeding great army."[26] He can, and He has done it.

St. Paul was no dreamer, yet he saw and understood that which for him turned death into life and life to death. For him this life was living death; death was the beginning of life. "Who will deliver me from the body of this death?" he cries; and he adds elsewhere: "I desire to be dissolved and to be."[27] He desired to be dissolved, not that he might end, but that he might begin; not that he might rest, but that he might labor; not that he might

[25] Heb. 9:27.
[26] Ezek. 37:10.
[27] Phil. 1:23.

look back on what he had done, but that he might look forward. No wonder he could cry in triumph, "Death, where is thy victory? Death, where is thy sting?"[28] For death had been swallowed up in his conquest.

And the same is true of very many. We have all watched them striding down the plane of time, laughing as they went, enjoying this life as only those can enjoy it who have no misgivings about the next. We have seen them nearing the goal, with their eyes fixed on the light beyond. When the time has come, they have been ready, and we have felt that indeed they were men.

Of everyone, young and old alike, death makes either a friend or an enemy. To his enemy, he is an abiding terror, to his friend he is a friend indeed; warning in danger, encouraging with strong hope in trial, reconciling in misfortune, stirring when action is called for, stimulating to every sacrifice.

[28] 1 Cor. 15:55.

Chapter 9

The Saints Show Us That Death
Is the Door to Eternal Life

There is one feature common to all the saints; perhaps it is common to all who approach to sanctity. One and all, they longed to die. We may not sympathize with their desire. We may think them somewhat exaggerated or mistaken. But the fact is written nevertheless in the life of every saint without exception. It was not so much because they were tired of this life, although most of them had in all conscience reason enough to know it and be weary. Neither was it because they had little fellow-feeling for their fellow-men, for no one knows the meaning of love, and no one proves it by deeds, better or more lavishly than a saint. Again, it was not because they were weary in themselves, and wished merely to rest from their labors. We have one saint saying he would gladly live on at any cost just to save a single soul more, and another who looked on the life beyond the grave as the life of the most intense labor.

No, the saints were none of them cowards; none of them were thin-skinned creatures. They did not shirk suffering or work; no one who knows them will accuse them of that. On the contrary, the more we know them, the more they stand out as the models of endurance and self-sacrifice. If ever a life of any one of them gives us a different impression, we know that it is untrue. In them at least the longing for death was not a drooping, disheartened thing; it was allied with a superhuman energy. They were indeed weary of this life, yet they served it with all their might. They longed every day to leave it, yet they lived it and labored in it as if it were the only thing worthy of their energies. This is but one more of the many paradoxes of sanctity. If we could but clearly understand it, we would discover the secret of Apostles.

And can we not? Surely it is not so difficult. The saints could hold their counsel when prudence or justice demanded it, but when God's glory was at stake, there was no one more willing to speak. If, then, we ask them to explain, perhaps they will make it clear.

Let us take two of them, so different yet so alike: St. Paul and St. Teresa. Whatever the differences between these two, they were at least alike in that they were utterly spontaneous and true, utterly devoid of any shadow of self-consciousness. When they spoke, their words came from the heart. Never, perhaps, has a writer more accurately portrayed himself and his thoughts than have these two.

How, then, does St. Paul explain himself? How does he reconcile his longing for death and his unbounded energy in this life? For we know that he longed for death. "Unhappy man that I am," he says in one place, "who will deliver me from the body of this death?" And in another: "I desire to be dissolved and to be with Christ." Of this at least the explanation was easy; it was because he saw and looked for more beyond. "We see now as in a glass after a dark manner," he says, "but then we shall see face-to-face."[29] And upon this he comments elsewhere: "Eye hath not seen, nor ear heard, neither hath it entered into the heart of

[29] See 1 Cor. 13:12.

man to conceive what things God hath prepared for them that love Him."[30] For them that love Him! "Then love Him I will," we seem to hear him say to himself; come what come may, nothing shall keep him from that. " I am sure that neither death, nor life, nor angels, nor principalities, nor powers, nor things present, nor things to come, nor might, nor height, nor depth, nor any other creature, shall be able to separate us from the love of God, which is in Christ Jesus our Lord."[31]

But love is a driving force. "The love of Christ compels me,"[32] he says once; and again another time: "Woe is unto me if I preach not the gospel."[33] Love drove him; love compelled him. The very prospect of what was yet to be, forced him to live this life the more. Love looked out through his eyes upon the world—love, which had seen the truth and which saw what this world might be if it would—and love can never stand still. "For which cause," he says, "we faint not.... For the things which are seen are temporal, but the things which are not seen are eternal.... And therefore we labor, whether absent or present, to please Him."[34] And how St. Paul did labor! Was ever a worker so keen?

"My little children," he cries to his Galatians who had hurt him, "of whom I am in labor again, until Christ be formed in you."[35] No, St. Paul's longing for death did not spoil his interest in life, and he tells us clearly enough the reason why.

Let us now turn to that other apostle, St. Teresa, whose fruits were so very many, although her methods were so very different.

[30] 1 Cor. 2:9.
[31] Rom. 8:38.
[32] 2 Cor. 5:14.
[33] 1 Cor. 9:16.
[34] 2 Cor. 4:16, 17; 5:9.
[35] Gal. 4:19.

She, too, longed for death; yet she, too, spent herself in a life of untold energy. Why the first? And what had it to do with the second? She tells us very plainly, and her words are but an echo of those of St. Paul. "I know a person," she says, speaking of herself, "who longed to die, not merely that she might at last see God, but that she might be freed from the constant torment that she felt because of her base ingratitude to Him to whom she was, and ever would be, so deeply indebted. It seemed to her that no one's faults would equal hers, because she knew that there was no one whom God had endured with so much patience, and on whom He had conferred so many favors."

So much she writes as she thinks of herself. But soon her thoughts turn to God and His goodness, and she says: "Because of these unspeakable favors, the soul burns with longing to enjoy Him who bestows them upon her, so that she lives in a great yet delightful torment, and is keen to die, and hence with continual tears does she beg of God that He would take her out of this exile."

Then at once, to show how this longing for death stirred the spirit of zeal within her, she goes on: "O poor butterfly! Thou art bound by many bonds which will not let thee fly as thou wilt. Have pity on her, O my God! Dispose everything here in such a manner that so even now she may in some degree satisfy the desire that she has for Thy honor and glory. Regard not her puny merits; consider not the baseness of her nature. Thou art able, O Lord, to bid the mighty sea stand back, and great Jordan divide, that the children of Israel may pass through.

"And yet do not pity her too much, for with Thy hand to help her, she will be able to endure many crosses. This she is determined to do; she has a longing desire to endure them. Extend, O Lord, Thy mighty arm. Let not her life be spent on things that are worthless. Let Thy greatness appear in this weakling woman, that men, who know she can endure nothing of herself, may be driven to praise Thee, cost what it may! This is the desire of her heart, and she would give a thousand lives, if she had them, that so a single soul might by her means praise Thee but a little more. For that gain she would hold them very well bestowed, for she knows full well that to suffer the very least cross for Thee, much less death itself, is far beyond anything she deserves."

So do the saints blend the two lives together. They make little of this life of time, not because in itself it is little, nor because they fail to grasp its attraction; not because they have been embittered, nor because they have shuddered at its cost; but because their eyes have been opened, and because, by comparison with the better thing, it is so small, so tawdry—a "gigantic falsehood," as St. Teresa elsewhere calls it. And yet again they make much of it; much more, when the total is summed up, than men of the world themselves make of it. For they have stood out of it, and so have seen it in its right perspective. They have put it in the scales against another life, and so have found its true value. They have breathed another air, a clearer atmosphere, and have been permeated with a new fire. When, then, they have been brought back to it and have been again confined within its prison, the craving that possesses them for the better will not be quieted, but must find satisfaction somewhere; and since they cannot reach that which is the best, they must needs go down among the things about them and lift them up, and make them like the best, and find a tempered relief in that.

A saint cannot count the cost; he cannot labor for a price. The thing itself made better is reward enough, if we speak of reward in his case. He gives, and esteems it a favor that he is allowed to give. He works because he is compelled to it. He has his eye and his heart on the life that alone can content him, and while it is deferred, he must make this life as much like the reality as he may.

Who has not felt, sometime, somewhere, at least a little of this enthusiasm? Who has not known from his own experience that this triumph of the saints is the summit of human nature? Who has not looked out upon some beautiful landscape and enjoyed it, and then in a moment discovered himself alien to it—in it but not of it, as a spirit from another world who had wandered into this? And in the moment that he so stood out of it, he has heard angels telling him that in that moment he was touching the naked truth of being, of which all this outer world was but the clothing. And when he has come back to the body of this death, he has hungered for that which has passed and has longed that all the world might see what he has seen.

And yet how little can we do! Poor little butterflies, how little can we do! But a butterfly is a thing of beauty, and the fairest of gardens is the fairer for its flitting presence. So at least we can do so much. At least we can live in the glory of God's sunlight; and men shall praise Him the more because we have been.

Chapter 10

You Receive Divine Life in the Blessed Sacrament

In the records left to us by the first missionaries among the American Indians, there is an ancient practice described that is much to our purpose here. In a certain tribe—the noblest-spirited that the Fathers had yet met—it was the custom when a great brave died to take the following means so that his name and memory might not perish. The chiefs and priests would gather together around the corpse, would invoke the guidance of the spirit of him who was dead, and then would choose out from the youth of the tribe one who gave good promise for the future, one who seemed both likely and willing to emulate the valor of the hero who was gone. He was brought into the middle of the village; he was told in detail all that the dead man had been and all that he had done—his fleetness of foot, his dexterity of hand, his prowess in hunting, his courage on the field of battle, his wisdom in council, his power of command, the awe with which he filled his enemies, his devotion to his tribe, and his sacrifice of himself for its sake. And when the tale had been told, the youth was asked whether he was willing to inherit the dead man's spirit, and to reproduce his life, and to pay the price of that reproduction.

And when the boy had sworn over the body of the dead that he would do this so far as in him lay, and that to give life and expression to that spirit should be the ambition of his life, then the oldest brave would stoop down to the corpse and cut out a portion of the heart, and put it on the tongue of the boy, and pray that by that act the spirit of the dead might pass into him, and in him find a new home. And forthwith the boy laid aside his own name, and received the name of the dead man. He stripped himself of his own clothing and put on the clothing of the dead. He passed out from his own family and was adopted into the family of the brave. Boy as he was, he was given a place in the Great Council of the tribe, because of the spirit that was now assumed to dwell in him. On the battlefield, he was given the place of honor, and that was the place of greatest danger. At home and abroad, it was assumed of him that he would sacrifice himself at any need.

Is there not some likeness between this Indian custom and the Christian's reception of the Blessed Sacrament? Yes, but with how great a difference! For the Chieftain whom we revere is no mere brave of a tribe, but Lord of Heaven and earth. He is not dead, but is risen again and alive. "If Christ be not risen, then is our faith in vain."[36] He has not passed away, but abides and will abide: "Jesus Christ, yesterday, today, and the same also forever."[37] And hence, our initiation is not a mere form; it is a solemn reality. We do not receive a portion of a dead man's heart, but a Heart that beats with quickened life. The spirit that passes into us is not a figure only; it is a real, living, quivering thing.

The full meaning of our words we do not know, for they are His words and not ours; but we do know that He has said: "He

[36] 1 Cor. 15:14.
[37] Heb. 13:8.

that eateth me, the same also shall live by me," for "my Body is meat indeed, and my Blood is drink in very deed."[38] We know that He has said: "If anyone love me, he will keep my word, and my Father will love him, and we will come to him, and will make our abode in him."[39] We know that "to as many as receive Him He has given power to become sons of God,"[40] and we know that one who understood the heart and soul of the God-man far better than we do has said, "Brethren, we are now the sons of God, but we know not what we shall be."[41]

And we believe, with a faith that is not only surmise, that all this is not mere metaphor, mere figure of speech, and no more. Such emphasis, if figure of speech only is intended, is not the manner of the Word of God. We believe that there are states of being far transcending our own, surpassing ours more than the moving creature surpasses the stone, than man surpasses the brute animal, than his immortal soul surpasses his mortal body. We believe that human language has been made to express the facts of human life; that it is therefore utterly inadequate to express the facts of a life that is above it; that often, then, its words must appear metaphorical and figurative when they are really attempts to utter the most solemn truths. And this is what we see to have happened here.

Man feebly guesses at the fact of the Blessed Sacrament and its life within the soul of man. He babbles words that express but a shadow; but the shadow they express is cast by a still greater reality. Although we do not understand, we know it must be true. When

[38] John 6:58, 56 (RSV = John 6:57, 55).
[39] John 14:23.
[40] John 1:12.
[41] See 1 John 3:2.

we adopt the name of Christ and call ourselves Christians, there is a real adoption corresponding to that name. Having received the living Body of Christ, there is a real meaning in our words when we say: "I live, now not I, but Christ lives in me."[42]

---

[42] Gal. 2:20.

Chapter 11

Holy Communion Unites You with Christ

There is an instinct in us all, no matter how unaccustomed we may
be to pray, that seems to tell us that if ever our prayer should be
real and from the depth of the soul, it should be so at the moment
of Holy Communion. If the Blessed Sacrament is that which, on
the authority of our Lord's own words, we believe it to be, His own
true Body and His own true Blood, there must be no imitation,
there must be no mere playing at devotion, there must be a strong
soul's genuine expression of itself, whenever we receive it into
ourselves. Hence, the universal custom of regular preparation for
Communion and regular thanksgiving after it, which in practice
are made of almost as much account as the receiving of the sacrament itself. Hence, too, the further common custom of spending
the first moments after Communion in intent contemplation, as
if we feared that the use of a book or of any other help to prayer
might be almost a desecration of a moment so solemn.

Undoubtedly the instinct is a good one, and both the resulting
practices are good. At the same time, as with all things good, the
importance of both can be exaggerated. Preparation and thanksgiving are very far from being the sacrament itself, while to one who is
wholly unaccustomed to contemplation, a book may help to prayer

when without it the soul will be wholly distracted. But not on that account should we decline to make the effort. Rightly understood, contemplation is less beyond our range than is sometimes assumed, and there are none who may not attain to it in some degree.

The following method of preparation and thanksgiving for Holy Communion is built upon this first principle. It is an easy form of contemplation. It is drawn from the three most elementary facts of Holy Communion. It is intended to be going on, no matter at what moment Communion is received, so that it is at once preparation and thanksgiving. It is reduced to the fewest possible words, for by many words, contemplation is often only distracted. Instead, it endeavors to take the affections that are immediately suggested, crystallizes them in a single sentence, and then offers them to the communicant to be held in the mind and meant by the heart for so long as mind and heart are able to retain them.

What, then, is Holy Communion? It contains three facts: the fact of Jesus Christ, its Substance; the fact of myself, its recipient; the fact of the union between Him and myself, from which Communion takes its name. These three facts make three points, and they contain enough, for they suggest affections that will stay.

The fact of Jesus Christ. The moment I say this to myself, meaning it, I make an act of faith. Hence, with St. John in the boat on Lake Tiberias I say, and repeat with even more realized meaning, "It is the Lord."[43] Or with the poor man appealing for his cure, "Lord, I believe; help Thou my unbelief."[44] Or with St. Peter, I can cry with my whole heart, "Thou art the Christ, the Son of the living God."[45]

---

[43] John 21:7.
[44] Mark 9:24.
[45] Matt. 16:16.

Knowledge is the forerunner of love. Of how many men and women is it said that to know them is to love them! And if this is true of ordinary mortals, how much truer must it be of our Lord! The act of faith, then, persisted in and meant, insensibly develops into an act of love. If we go on saying and meaning, "Lord, I believe," we shall soon find ourselves saying, "Lord, I love." So in the words of Peter let my thoughts express themselves: "Lord, Thou knowest that I love Thee. Thou knowest all things; Thou knowest that I love Thee."[46] Or with the spouse in the Canticle: "I to my Beloved, and my Beloved to me."[47] Or I can keep the words of à Kempis echoing in my heart: "Love Him, and keep Him for thy Friend who, when all leave thee, will not forsake thee, nor suffer thee to perish in the end."[48]

But when I say this, I find my act of love is insensibly going a step farther. As knowledge leads to love, so love expresses itself in confidence and trust. As, then, an act of faith leads insensibly to an act of love, so an act of love falls naturally into an act of hope. Hence, once again with St. Peter we say, "Lord, to whom shall we go? Thou hast the words of eternal life."[49] or with the psalmist, "The Lord is my Shepherd; whom shall I fear? The Lord is the keeper of my soul; before whom shall I tremble?"[50] Or with the writer of the *Te Deum*: "In Thee, O Lord, I have hoped; I shall not be confounded forever."

The fact of myself. What a contrast! What an opposite extreme! In circumstances such as these, in associations such as these, how inevitable is the act of humility, of self-abasement, whether saying with St. Elizabeth, "Whence is this to me that my Lord should

---

[46] John 21:16, 17.
[47] Cant. 6:2 (RSV = Song of Sol. 6:2).
[48] Thomas a Kempis, Imitation of Christ, Bk. 2, ch. 7.
[49] John 6:69 (RSV = John 6:68).
[50] See Ps. 22:1, 26:1 (RSV = Ps. 23:1, 27:1).

come to me?"[51] or with the soldier, "Lord, I am not worthy that Thou shouldst enter under my roof,"[52] or with the psalmist, "What is man that Thou shouldst be mindful of him or the son of man that Thou shouldst visit him?"[53]

Not only of my nature am I, who am but dust and ashes, and, even at my best, but the work of His hands, compelled to humble myself before our Lord. I am lower down than that. I have lowered myself still more by misuse of that which He has made, by infidelity to Him, by sinfulness. In this way and that I have offended Him and soiled myself. So, as I approach Him, I can only say, "Lord, be merciful to me a sinner."[54] Or with the prodigal, "Father, I have sinned against Heaven and in Thy sight. I am no longer worthy to be called Thy son."[55] Or, in the words of the *Miserere*, "Have mercy on me, O God, according to Thy great mercy."[56]

And yet, even while I speak, "while I am yet a great way off,"[57] He, like the father of the prodigal, comes to me and embraces me. This is the matter of fact; unworthy as I am, stained as I am and in rags, He will take me as I am if I will come. So I cannot refuse. I can only say, "Take, O Lord, and receive all my liberty."[58] I can only cry, "Into Thy hands, O Lord, I commend my spirit."[59] I can only plead, offering myself to Him in the meantime: "Lord, he whom Thou lovest is sick."[60]

[51] Luke 1:43.
[52] Matt. 8:8.
[53] Ps. 8:5 (RSV = Ps. 8:4).
[54] See Luke 18:13.
[55] Luke 15:21.
[56] Ps. 50:3 (RSV = Ps. 51:1).
[57] Luke 15:20.
[58] Prayer of St. Ignatius of Loyola.
[59] Luke 23:46.
[60] John 11:3.

The fact of the union. This is the climax. My Lord and I are brought together, made actually one, so far as that is possible. It is not to be wondered at that, at that moment, words seem to fail us. We can only adore, and adoration is best expressed by silence. Our thoughts can only repeat, with St. Thomas, "My Lord and my God";[61] or the words of the *Te Deum*: "Thou, O Christ, art the King of Glory," or with the other St. Thomas: "Hidden Godhead, devoutly I adore Thee."

When at length, as it were, I recover my power of speech, and my heart longs to express itself, what else can it do but break out in words of thanksgiving? It says with the priest in the Mass, "What return shall I make to the Lord for all He has given to me?"[62] Or, "We praise Thee; we bless Thee; we adore Thee; we glorify Thee; we give Thee thanks." Or, again, in the words of St. Paul: "Christ loved me, and gave Himself up for me."[63]

But there is no gratitude, no proof of confidence, greater than that which makes further appeals; and even while I thank Him for all that He is, and for all that He has done, I seem to hear Him say, "Hitherto you have asked nothing in my name. Ask and you shall receive, that your joy may be filled."[64] So I turn my prayer, or my prayer turns itself, to one of petition—that I myself may do His will: "Lord, what wilt Thou have me to do?";[65] that His will may be done in and by all His creatures, "Hallowed be Thy name. Thy kingdom come; Thy will be done on earth as it is in Heaven"; and that if

---

[61] John 2:28.
[62] See Ps. 115:12 (RSV = Ps. 116:12).
[63] Gal. 2:20.
[64] John 16:24.
[65] Acts 9:6.

this thing or that, this favor or that, dear to my heart, for myself or for another, is in accordance with His will, it may be granted.

Hence, the form here suggested will be summed up as follows: What is Holy Communion?

It is the fact of Jesus Christ, which implies:

An act of faith: "It is the Lord." "Lord, I believe, help Thou my unbelief." "Thou art the Christ, the Son of the living God."

An act of love: "Lord, Thou knowest all things; Thou knowest that I love Thee." "I to my Beloved, and my Beloved to me." "Love Him, and keep Him for thy Friend, who, when all leave thee, will not forsake thee, nor suffer thee to perish in the end."

An act of hope: "Lord, to whom shall we go? Thou hast the words of eternal life." "The Lord is my Shepherd; whom shall I fear? The Lord is the keeper of my soul; before whom shall I tremble?" "In Thee, O Lord, I have hoped; I shall not be confounded forever."

It is the fact of myself. This evokes:

An act of humility: "Whence is this to me, that my Lord should come to me?" "Lord, I am not worthy that Thou shouldst enter under my roof." "What is man that Thou shouldst be mindful of him, or the son of man that Thou shouldst visit him?"

An act of contrition: "Lord, be merciful to me, a sinner." "Father, I have sinned against Heaven and in Thy sight; I am no longer worthy to be called Thy son." "Have mercy on me, O God, according to Thy great mercy."

An act of oblation: "Take, O Lord, and receive all my liberty." "Into Thy hands, O Lord, I commend my spirit." "Lord, he whom Thou lovest is sick."

It is the fact of the union, which draws forth:

An act of adoration: "My Lord and my God." "Thou, O Christ, art the King of Glory." "Hidden Godhead, devoutly I adore Thee."

An act of thanksgiving: "What return shall I make to the Lord for all He has given to me?" "We praise Thee; we bless Thee; we adore Thee; we glorify Thee; we give Thee thanks." "Christ loved me, and gave Himself up for me."

An act of petition: "Lord, what wilt Thou have me to do?" "Hallowed be Thy name. Thy kingdom come; Thy will be done on earth as it is in Heaven."

This is, of course, no more than a suggestion and a guide. The variety of acts that each might make for himself is very great; the brief prayers that might be given are infinite. And as every soul is different, so will each have its own form of self-expression. Let it choose as it will and pray in the way it finds best.

Chapter 12

The Lord Needs Workers to Lead Souls to Him

We have all known many men who do many striking and noteworthy things, attain the height of their ambition, win for themselves a great and even worthy name, and yet feel when the goal had been reached that somehow they had failed, somehow they were disappointed, somehow they had not done that with their lives for which their lives were made. On the other hand, none of us has ever known a man to save a soul and regret it; none of us has ever known a man even work to save a soul, whether he succeeded in saving it or not, and think that his time has been misspent.

I have known an eminent mathematician who said he would give all he knew to be able to preach a single sermon that would really reach down into a single soul; an eminent university professor who, the more the world of intellect smiled upon him, felt all the more that to serve a human soul was a greater honor; an eminent artist, who gloried in his art, not for the reputation that it brought him, nor even for the art's own sake, but solely because it had become in his hands a means of rescuing and lifting up the lives of others.

And surely these are not rare exceptions. Is there a man in all the world with a mind that understands and a heart that feels and common sense to guide his judgment who does not appreciate the good thing it is to keep another man from harm? Is there a man who has not a longing to do something good for someone else before he dies; nay, more, who does not know that if he can gain this, more than if he gains any other thing that he ambitions, then his life will find its satisfaction?

We look at men around us; sometimes we feel a sort of envy for those who prosper where we fail and who rise to great heights before the eyes of others. When time is past, and history is written, and men are arranged in the order of their real worth, we do not esteem the rich men most, nor the prosperous, nor the powerful, nor the learned, but the men who have been true in themselves and have given their lives for the service and saving of others. The rest come next, not in the order of their wealth, or their power, or their learning, but according to the use they have made of these accidental gifts of God for the good of their fellows.

And as we judge the past, so do we judge the future. Wealth and power and learning may be important matters, but the man that will stoop to lift up his fellowman is greater than them all. He will be the force that will tell through all time and in every crisis and will find for himself the satisfaction of a life well spent that nothing else will give him.

There are few men who do not know this in their hearts. There are many who would like and would be willing, if they but knew how, to make it the ruling motive of their lives. They would give themselves to the service if they could; they would labor if they could. If they could, they would be willing—indeed, who could be a man and yet would be unwilling to go out and lift up a soul that was stifling in the mire? At least, there are few who at some time or another in their lives have not had this attraction. But some have thought it was not for them and have suffered it to perish. Their circumstances have been against them. They have had themselves to consider. They have had the cares of this world put upon them. Others have reckoned up the cost, and have found it a dear one to pay. Others, again, have had the dream and dwelled upon it, but with them it has never come to action; it has remained a dream and no more and, like other dreams, has gradually vanished beyond recall. They have forgotten the ideal in the fancied real; they have allowed the present interest, perhaps the present need, to blot out the greater thing that might have been. And they have satisfied themselves that this was enough; this is all for which they were made. They were not made to save the souls of others; that requires a special vocation; it is enough if they can save their own.

We do not say this in blame. Many, perhaps, would do something if they could; many would still answer if they heard the Master's obvious call. But the fact remains; meanwhile the work grows every day greater, and the recruits for the army of our Lord stand still. Every day the world grows larger and more open; every day there are more souls offered to be saved; yet every day, by comparison at least, there seem to be fewer and fewer men at hand to save them. Never before in the history of the human race has the man who would work for the saving of others had such an opportunity as now. At home and abroad, in civilized and in savage countries, the whole earth is gaping, parched, and dry; and it cannot be moistened except by the sweat of the laborer's brow, if not by the blood from his veins. Not only is today the laborer's day; it is also the season for ingathering. The seed has been long sown; the blood that should water it has been long shed. Others have labored for centuries in patience and failure, and now we have but to lift our eyes and see the fields white for the harvest.

Overcoming Worldly Concerns

At home on every side the cry is heard: "Had we more priests we could stop the leakage. Had we more priests there are countless numbers of our countrymen ready to come in."

From the mission fields, it is the same. "Send us priests," they appeal. "We have souls without number for them to save." Never does a missionary come home who is not struck with the work that might be done if only the men would go out and do it. For the men are here, and the work is waiting there; would to God they could be brought together!

This is the appeal that rings out to all the world; but especially, here and now, should it echo throughout Great Britain. Once it was the day for Spain, once for Portugal, once for France; each in its turn has had the world beneath its feet. And they produced upon demand the men who were required, their Xaviers and their Clavers, their Silveiras and their Machados, their Jogues, and their Brébeufs—men of whom today their fellow countrymen are proud, as those who gave themselves to save their country's honor in the days of its prosperity, and luxury, and danger of disgrace. Now the wheel has turned, and the day has come for us. Let us not stay to lament that Britain is not Catholic; let us not despair at the smallness of our numbers. Whether our numbers are great or small, each of us still is one; and if we are so few, why, then, "the fewer men, the greater share of honor."

That not mere number makes the difference the past has clearly shown. It is not number, but willingness; not learning, but self-sacrifice; not even any special skill or training, but a strong desire to spread the kingdom, a strong hand to put to the plough.

Shall we, then, be wanting? Fathers and mothers, I care not who you are, rich or poor, noble or lowly, do you really grudge to God one or even more of the sons whom He has given to you? Is it such a mean thing, as some would seem to think it, that a son of theirs should hold their Maker in his hands, should plead for them and for others at the altar, should be called upon to tramp down a sodden street, or across a veldt, or through a jungle, to carry salvation to a single soul? All honor to the widowed mother of five sons, who gave them all to God and has lived to see them die one by one, priest-victims on the mission fields!

Sons and daughters, is there any ambition that is nobler? When you come to die, would you regret it if there were souls in Heaven waiting there to thank you for the gift of life you had given them? Other treasures you must leave behind; this is yours, if you will have it, for all eternity. And even if this world's estimate be taken, what life will you find more worthy of, more suited to, the energy and talents that are yours? Luxury, I grant you, you will not have; but you shall have even here a hundredfold instead. Mere wealth will never be yours; but love is more than gold or silver, and it you shall have to overflowing. Honor from men you may or may not receive; instead, centuries hence, when this generation is forgotten, the work you have done will still live on, and somewhere someone will bless the unknown hand that was generous; that gave and did not count the cost; that toiled and did not seek for rest; that labored and did not look for any reward, save only to know that it worked for the glory of God and the good of the souls of men.

Chapter 13

Christ Has Influenced the World
More Than Any Other Person

Explain it as we will, in the history of the world, one influence
stands out as unique. There have been many great and good men;
there have been some founders of great and permanent move-
ments—religious, political, and moral; great ideas have been started,
great principles enunciated, which have altered the whole course
of civilization and thought. But no single man, no single idea, has
so revolutionized the world, its trend of life, and its interpretation
of itself as the person and teaching of Jesus Christ. A few would
class Him with other reformers; they know that by so doing, they
deprive Him of His due. He stands alone. "*Anno Domini*—the year
of the Lord," is no accidental and convenient means of dating; we
do not speak of the year of Confucius, or the year of Buddha, or
the year of Luther, or the year of Napoleon. It stands for a great
upheaval, greater than any that these have made. It stands for the
coming of One who has transcended all others in His teaching,
and in the effect His teaching has produced, and therefore who
surpasses all others in His life and being.

But that is not the whole of the matter. It is not even the most
important part. Not only does the present state of man upon the

earth drive me back to a point at which, and to a person in whom, the whole human race began again, but the momentum of that revolution is evidently not yet spent. In spite of the many backwaters, in spite of countless reactions, that force which is understood by Christianity has never worn out—indeed, was never stronger than now. To deny this, or even to ignore it, is a greater folly than to deny the fact of Christ Himself. And to this there is no parallel at all. Do what its enemies will, this faith in Jesus Christ goes everywhere, permeates everything, and rouses slumbering embers today as much as ever it did, more than ever it did, in any generation before. Is a new country opened up? The followers of Christ pierce into it, if, indeed, they are not found to have anticipated the explorer. Is a new nation formed? Every day, in proportion to its growth in greatness, does its Christianity grow. Is a new philosophy thought out? Immediately it is tested on the anvil of Christianity. Does a new enemy of law and order lift its head? The one and immediate object of its attack is the fact of Jesus Christ and the Spirit He has sent into the world.

We go back, then, to examine this beginning, and here the discovery is still more startling. Given the most stirring description of this Christ that His most devoted follower has drawn—given, if you like, the most exaggerated picture that the stoutest enthusiast has painted—what an insignificant cause it offers to explain so stupendous an effect! To say that the movement had none but a fancied founder is portentous enough; to say that this and no more was the founder seems almost more portentous. And yet it is the matter of fact. Whichever way I turn, however I may search, whatever explanation I may devise, all my paths converge upon this common center. I may accept it, or I may leave it. I have no other escape. If I leave it, I do violence to my reason, and to all my first principles of knowledge; if I accept it, whatever consequences may follow in its train, however hard may be their details, I am at least consistent with all my other axioms of thought. Startling as it may appear, impossible as it may seem, an unknown carpenter of an unknown village, who wrote no books, who built no monument, who assembled no army, who conquered no country, who founded no school, who developed no philosophy, who made no addition to science, who invented no machinery, who explored no strange land, the most noteworthy event of whose life was the fact that He died a convict's death, has been the reformer of the world—nay, more, is the world's reformer today.

Evidently, then, whether I see it or not, there is something in this Christ more than appears, something behind, whatever there may be outside. In shape and behavior I see Him to be as other men. He eats and drinks, He grows and matures, He works and rests, like the rest of us; there is that in His speech and in His manner so entirely ordinary, common, that He is classed as insignificant by those who knew Him best, and they were only village laborers. And yet with all this insignificance, there is no man more noticed than He.

He is noticed so as to make many friends. Wherever He goes, into whatever city, among whatever class, among rich and poor, innocent and sinful, learned and ignorant, rulers and ruled, He has some who make Him their all-in-all. In His own age, in every age since, and in our own, whether or not men deny Christ Himself, they cannot deny the unbroken line of His friends, who have lived for Him, have labored for Him, have died for Him, have found their one glory in Him—a line to which there is no end, and in comparison with which there is no parallel.

And he is noticed, on the other hand, so as to make many enemies. If Christ had always, and still has, the longest line of friends, He has the largest number of enemies also. "Behold, all the world goes after Him," in the one company or in the other. He who is not with Him is against Him;[66] there is no neutral attitude possible.

What is it that makes this difference? What else can it be but something that sets Him apart from all others? This Jesus Christ, if He has done what He has done, if He is what He is, is not merely unique among men. He is, He must be, something more than man. Then what is He? What is that being which never dies? What is that life which so outpours itself and yet is never exhausted? "Jesus Christ, yesterday, today, and the same forever,"[67] was said of Him two thousand years ago; the same is said of Him still. They are shut up in a deep and dark cavern who think it is not so. When we are dead and gone, and the best and greatest of us is forgotten, when His enemies are dead and gone, and all their ammunition has been spent, it will continue to be said of Him: He will still be the force that will count, for the resurrection and for the fall of many, and for a sign to be contradicted;[68] still will He be making friends, still making enemies. At times the world will recover itself and own Him, and will rejoice and be glad and go forward in the knowledge. At times and in places—although never wholly, as it has never done—it will go backward and disown Him, and those will be days of falsehood and unrest. But in either case, it will always be, as it has always been since He came, the acceptance or the rejection of this Christ, this obviously living Christ, that will characterize every succeeding generation and every soul that it contains.

Once more, then, who and what is this Christ? This is not the argument. Strictly speaking, it is not one of the arguments by

[66] See Matt. 12:30.
[67] Heb. 13:8.
[68] See Luke 2:34.

which the divinity of Christ is proven, but surely it is one of the signs by which it is manifested. It is not the argument by which we show that, having loved His own who were in the world, He has loved them unto the end,[69] but surely it compels us to cry out: "Behold how He has loved."[70] It is not the basis commonly given of the heroism of the saints; but surely it is the secret of their superhuman strength and the fulfillment of that promise: "Behold, I am with you all days, even to the consummation of the world."[71] And if so, it justifies that portentous charge "Go, therefore, and teach all nations,"[72] and it explains that commission's fulfillment.

What no human power could have done, the divine Man of Nazareth has effected. What the mightiest of emperors with his legions could not hope for has been accomplished by a band of fishermen, with this divine Leader at their head. What today combined science and learning, armies and navies, alliances and agreements would not dream of taking in hand, that same is being carried through before our every eyes by the unknown disciples of this unknown Master, without money to help them, without a sword to defend them, in almost every unknown corner of the world. And when present empires have passed away, and the learning of our time has come to be smiled at as old-world simplicity, the work they are now doing will still abide and will still be spread by others fired with the same unutterable craving that He may be known and loved and served.

To know this Jesus Christ as He is now, living, and active, and fascinating by His perfect self, not merely as He was in the days of

[69] John 13:1.
[70] See John 11:36.
[71] Matt. 28:20.
[72] Matt. 28:19.

His pilgrimage: this is the secret of the saints. For to know Him is now, as it was then, either to love Him or to hate Him; to love Him with a boundless love, or to hate Him unto death. It is a matter of proportion. The man who says he neither loves nor hates, does not yet know Jesus Christ as He is. That which he knows is but a shadow, but a feeble imitation of the truth; the true Jesus Christ compels. "The love of Christ drives me," says the apostle St. Paul;[73] it drives every man who comes within its thrall, and it is a thraldom whose yoke is sweet and whose burden is a glory.

[73] See 2 Cor. 5:14.

Chapter 14

You Must Choose between Good and Evil

That these are right and wrong, good and evil, of some kind, and that these are opposed to one another, all men are agreed. They agree, too, that in the end, right and good make for the benefit of the race, wrong and evil for its undoing. Some would go so far as to say that this constitutes their very definition. The man who acts rightly and does good is a blessing to his fellowmen; the man who acts wrongly and does evil is, in so far, a curse. Much more, then, if there is a common source of good and right, is it the source of all blessing to men; if there is a common source of evil and wrong, it is the plague-spot of creation.

This accepted principle is at the root of all our criminal code; it is at the root of all our treatment of evil-doing. When we condemn a convict to servitude extending over a length of years, we think of him more as a source of future anger than merely as a man who has done wrong and must be punished. When we hang a murderer, it is more because he is, as we call him, a danger to society, than because of the actual evil he has done. And so in many other ways we act upon the assumed axiom: the doer of evil, be he man or be he devil, is the enemy of the human race.

Overcoming Worldly Concerns

But although men are commonly agreed as to the principle, they are by no means at one as to its interpretation. Although we acknowledge the doer of evil to be the enemy of the race, it is not always clear what good and evil actually are. In the whole world as we know it, is there anything more desperate than the seemingly universal antagonism on this point? What to one man is an act of virtue, to another is a crime. One will hail as martyrdom what another will call a death of ignominy and shame. A saint will be persecuted on the holiest of grounds. The noblest of causes will be represented to some as the limit of disgrace. So it seems to have always been, so it is today; so, except for one gleam of hope, we might assume that it will be to the end. Agreed as the whole world is in principle, the seed of discord seems to be sown that will set good against good as long as time shall last, while evil battens on the victims of the fight. A good Mohammedan will massacre good Christians; a good Protestant will hang, draw, and quarter good Catholics; a good Inquisitor will condemn a good Jew to be burned; and each in doing so will, as our Lord foretold, think he is doing a service to God.

Can it be that this is intended? Can it be that while goodness is always, and in the minds of all, one and the same thing, nevertheless good men, good principles, good aims should always be opposed to and persecutors of each other? Or is there not some explanation that is other than goodness itself? May it not be possible that good is opposed to good, not because it is good, but because there is evil mixed with it, on one side or the other or both? May it not be that the crop that is growing is not wholly wheat, that an enemy has sown cockle among it, and that for the sake of the good the Master suffers both to grow together?[74]

[74] See Matt. 13:24-30.

Certainly, so long as things are human, they will not be wholly perfect; and, in our present state of being, this will imply a defect of some kind or other. Indeed, is not this the whole problem of a man's life? If things were wholly good or wholly bad, if their goodness or badness were written on their surface, then choice would be an easy matter. Even then a man could please himself; he could still choose good or evil; but if he chose evil, it would be without a shadow of excuse. As things are, it is different. Nothing in the world is so wholly bad that it cannot be given an appearance of good; nothing is so wholly good that it cannot be shown to be evil.

So, then, I am driven to this conclusion: If I am to distinguish between right and wrong, good and evil, I must not be content with appearances, with that which is shown upon the surface; I must go back to the broader principle, and I must go beyond to the ultimate issue. Evil is the enemy of the human race; so, however attractive a thing in itself may be, however at the moment it may plead for acceptance and approval, if it is injurious in its source, if its effects are inevitably injurious, it should have no part with me. Good, on the other hand, is always and invariably the ultimate friend of man; so, however a thing may be maligned, however lowly and despicable it may appear, if it comes from a good source, if it points to a good end, if it has always left good fruit behind it, it should be mine. Upon this basis, not upon that of my immediate circumstances, I must choose if I would choose as a man. The more I judge by that which is immediately around me, the more likely I am to be deceived. No man, says the proverb, is a judge in his own case. But if I will transcend these, if I will look at good and evil as they are, whence they come, whither they tend, and what are their real effects, I shall see and understand; then I shall be in less danger of deception.

For of the one and the other the effects are not far to seek, and by their effects, more than in any other way, we are told by our Lord we may know them.[75] Evil, first of all, is a deceiver; the Devil, says our Lord again, is a liar from the beginning.[76] Evil cannot possibly win the heart of any man except under the garb of good, for the heart of man in itself is good, and is drawn by good, however prone it may be to be seduced. Evil, then, must first lie to save its face; it must call itself a savior when it is a curse, a benefactor when its gifts are only plagues. But once it has found a foothold, then we may know it as it is. No tyrant is more tyrannical than evil; it will proclaim the reign of freedom and impose it upon its subjects at the point of the sword. No confusion is more confounded or confounding than evil; it will extol liberty of thought, will call for light and learning, but will tolerate no thought that differs from its own, will extinguish every light that is not to its fancy. It will go abroad as the champion of law and order, yet it will always leave behind it the marks of bondage, victories shouting with it the arrival of a golden age yet clanking their chains as the accompaniment to their song. There is no slavery like the slavery of evil. It saps the very desire of freedom; it blinds the eyes until they can see no other light; it stalks alongside like a hideous specter, terrifying its drunken victims until they dare not look to right or to left.

And there is the other side—thank God, the side that in the end appeals to the heart of every man. It is the side of Him who is "all things to all men,"[77] who has made Himself man's equal and not his master, or his master but that He might serve man the more, who has no lofty throne of majesty upon this earth, who lives in

[75] See Matt. 7:20.
[76] See John 8:44.
[77] See 1 Cor. 9:22.

lowliness, whose aspect is fair and winning, whose name, indeed, is so great that every knee must bow before it, and yet when we meet Him, we find He is "only Jesus."[78]

His is the other side, the side opposed to that of "the enemy of the human race," and the side that in every generation wins through to victory, even though it seems to be ever on the verge of defeat. And this side, too, cannot help but spread itself abroad. This world can never again be the place it was, once Christ our Lord has walked upon it; for even if He had spoken never a word, even if He had worked no miracle, virtue went out from Him as and wherever He walked. So is it with His followers. Let them only be like their Master, like Him in meekness, like Him in lowliness, like Him in aspect fair and winning, and they will need neither force nor falsehood to help them to conquer the hearts of men. "Blessed are the meek, for they shall possess the land."[79]

The two camps are pitched, and in one or the other every man must be enrolled. Every man's life must add its little quota to the side of good or evil; to the side of Christ, the sovereign God, or to the side of the enemy of the human race. The camps are pitched, the battle is raging, and mankind is the prize. And what a strange battle it is! For it is one not only of army against army, but of every single man against himself. We look through the fire and smoke and see every man dogged with his own particular devil. We see that by nature every man is good, in principle, in ideal, in intention; but at his side crouches a second self, a devil if we like to call him so, who vitiates his nature, who misapplies his principles, who corrupts his ideals, and who lulls his good intentions to sleep. And when he has done this, he persuades him that this state is better

[78] Matt. 17:8.
[79] Matt. 5:4.

than the first, that this is the reality and the other only a dream, that now he has found peace, or, at all events, as much as can be hoped for, and that those who think otherwise are wrong and must be suppressed. So he turns his arms against his own.

Poor blinded human nature! You were made for better things than this. And they are yours still if you will have them — if, that is, you will stand up and fight on their side.

Chapter 15

Christ's Words in the Gospel Speak to You Today

To all of us who are grown up, to most of us who are still growing up, there have come times when we have found the service of God no easy matter. To be steadily faithful to Him in our prayers, to keep His commandments as we know He would have us keep them, and to keep them from day to day without yielding for a moment: these are no light undertakings; without His grace to help us, they would be impossible.

And when these hours of trial have come, perhaps the thought has occurred to us that if only we could have lived in the lifetime and in the company of our divine Savior, if even now we could only see Him for a moment as He is, it might have been, and it might be, so much easier. A word from Him had power to break the heart of a hardened sinner like the Magdalene. If we could have heard that word with our own ears, perhaps we would have sinned so much less, perhaps we would have been so much more penitent. A single glance of His truth-compelling eyes forced hot tears of repentance from Peter; if we could only feel those eyes upon us, it might be so much easier to understand Him, so much easier to love Him, so much easier to give ourselves to His service.

And yet it must be remembered there is another side to the picture. Even of those who had this privilege, and they were many, the number who recognized and acknowledged Him was small. Many saw His wonderful works; many felt the influence of His words. Yet they followed Him, as He was forced to tell them, not because of Himself, but because of what He gave them, and in the hour of trial they fell away. "Amen, amen, I say to you," He said on one occasion. "You seek me, not because you have seen miracles, but because you did eat of the loaves and were filled."[80] Even His own disciples, who had been with Him from the beginning, who had seen all that He had done, had drunk in all the sweetness of His words, had learned to love the eager glancing of His eyes, had gone so far as to profess that, even if all the world forsook Him, they would not, even they could not stand the trial of the Crucifixion. "Then the disciples all leaving Him, fled away."[81]

"He was in the world, and the world was made by Him, and the world knew Him not. He came unto His own, and His own received Him not."[82] Are we, then, sure that we would have stood by Him? Are we sure that we would not have come under that bitter complaint pronounced by our Lord against His generation: "Having eyes, they see not, and having ears they do not hear, nor do they understand"?[83] After all, it may be better for us that we can look upon Him and study Him only at a distance.

We cannot, indeed, now with our own eyes "see the things"[84] that the disciples saw, but we have a picture, a portrait of those

[80] John 6:26.
[81] Mark 14:50.
[82] John 1:10-11.
[83] See Matt. 13:14-15.
[84] See Matt. 13:14-15.

things in our keeping. And as a portrait of an absent friend keeps his memory fresh with us, so the picture of our living Lord, "ever living to make intercession for us,"[85] brings Him to our mind—nay, more, if we study it carefully, may stir us to an even greater affection and devotion. Let us look at this picture for a minute and renew an old acquaintance.

We are walking along a country lane in the fertile upland of Galilee. The hills rise up on either side, green with pasture; the valley between teems with corn. There are men laboring in the fields, shepherds tending their sheep along the hillside, men and women here and there along the road. Presently, at a turn in the road, we come upon a group made up, for the most part, of simple country folk from the farms and cottages about. In the middle is a young man, tall and lithe in appearance, with an eastern turban on His head, His attire of white, and with a mantle over His shoulder. He is seated on a stone by the roadside and is talking quietly, but with words that are clearly full of interest to the simple folk gathered around Him. In His eyes there is a strange glitter, a mixture as of joy and pain, of laughter and tears, of hope and disappointment, which cannot be described. And over all is a cloak of enduring gentleness: gentleness in His eyes, gentleness over all His face, gentleness in the movement of His hands, which are resting on the heads of little children who have crept close to Him; gentleness, instinctive and therefore very true, in the order of His thoughts, in the tone of His voice, in the deliberation of His actions—this is the one leading feature of the picture.

We take up His words, and they have the same tale to tell: "Come to me, all you that labor and are burdened," He says, "I will refresh you. Take my yoke upon you, for my yoke is sweet and my burden light. And learn of me, because I am meek and humble of heart; and you shall find rest for your souls."[86]

He points to the sheep gathering around their shepherd on the hillside and says, "I am the Good Shepherd, and I know mine and mine know me ... and I lay down my life for my sheep."[87] He hears the shepherd call his flock together and sees him lead them to a fresh pasture, and He adds, "My sheep hear my voice, and I know them, and they follow me. And I give them life everlasting; and they shall not perish forever, and no man shall pluck them out of my hand."[88]

He points to the bright sun overhead, filling the valley with light and glory, and He says, "I am the light of the world; he that followeth me walketh not in darkness, but shall have the light of life."[89] He looks along the road that leads to the city in the distance and cries: "I am the way, the truth, and the life."[90] He sees the simple folk around Him with their simple food and tells them, "I am the Bread of Life: he that cometh to me shall not hunger, and he that believeth in me shall never thirst."[91]

And then He will go on to teach them how they, too, should imitate His enduring gentleness. "As often as you do it to the least of these my little ones," He says, as the little children clamber on His knee—"as often as you have given a cup of water to the least of these my little ones, you have given it to me."[92]

---

[86] Matt. 11:28-30.
[87] John 10:14.
[88] John 10:27-28.
[89] John 8:12.
[90] John 14:6.
[91] John 6:35 (RSV = John 6:34).
[92] Matt. 10:42.

"Love your enemies; do good to them that injure you and persecute you; and your reward shall be very great in Heaven."[93] Gentleness, forgivingness, He tells them, is the nature of God the Father, and He repeats to them the story of the Prodigal Son.[94] Gentleness, forgivingness, is His own nature, and He proves it by the story of the Good Shepherd. And gentleness, forgivingness, He would have to be the nature of every Christian, and He brings this lesson home by the story of the Good Samaritan.[95]

Presently He rises and passes through the group that presses close around Him. He seems to know them all. He has a kindly word for everyone. Obviously, all are dear to Him, for His interest is not official and no more. There they are, poor country-folk from the hillsides who have left the plough to listen to Him; poor laborers from the town who find in Him relief from unrest; poor fishermen from Galilee who have left their nets and their boats to share His lot. There are the lame and the blind, the deaf and the dumb, even the sick from the neighboring cottages. What a motley congregation! What a weird group on which to waste so finished a work of art as that discourse! But He does not think of that. He gives what He has, to anyone who will have it. As He passes along, one He will touch with His gentle hand, and will heal him; to another He will merely speak some word of comfort, and the sufferer will learn that which turns his pain into delight; to a third He will grant a favor greater than was asked for, and will say, "Son, go in peace, thy sins are forgiven thee."[96] But to whomsoever He speaks, no matter how few words He utters, whomsoever He

---

[93] See Matt. 5:44, 12.
[94] Luke 15:11-32.
[95] Luke 10:25-37.
[96] See Mark 2:5.

touches, no matter whether He heals them or not, all alike know the consolation of His presence and are contented with their lot for His sake. "And they all did wonder," St. Mark tells us, "saying: He hath done all things well; He hath made the deaf to hear, and the dumb to speak."[97]

It is not possible to make too much of this enduring gentleness of Jesus Christ. So kind was He that strong men were tempted to despise Him, as did Simon the Pharisee.[98] So gentle was He that His own disciples complained, as did Judas Iscariot, and "all with him."[99] So enduring was He, and in consequence so varied was the company He drew around Him that His enemies called out against Him as the comrade of drunkards and sinners. And such is the Jesus Christ who lives on today; the same, but, if possible, with a yet wider sympathy and feeling. For the arm of the Lord is not shortened. Having once risen, He dieth now no more;[100] and that same enduring gentleness marked the risen Jesus Christ as much as, more than, it marked Him before His death. That same Lord stands still in our midst, with us "all days, even to the consummation of the world,"[101] ever living to make intercession for us, ever healing, ever forgiving, ever making the same appeal to us for our affection in return — with the certainty of our faith we know it.

"Blessed are the eyes that see the things which you see. For I say to you that many prophets and kings have desired to see the things that you see and have not seen them, and to hear the things that

---

[97] Mark 7:37.
[98] See Luke 7:36-50.
[99] See John 12:4-5.
[100] Rom. 6:9.
[101] Matt. 28:20.

you hear, and have not heard them."[102] At the beginning, we were tempted to envy the Jews of Palestine. Do we ever think of those who envy us for what we see, and perhaps with greater reason? How many thousands, how many millions, are there who desire to see the things that we see, and to hear the things that we hear, and who, if they did see and hear, would turn what they learned to better account!

[102] Luke 10:23-24.

Chapter 16

Jesus Christ Is Fully Human

There is one aspect of the Gospel story that must strike any careful student. The fundamental fact of our Faith is that Jesus Christ our Lord is very God, yet the special object of the Gospels seems rather to be to emphasize the fact that He is very Man. He has gone out of His way, if we may put it so, to make us feel and know that He is one with us.

He preferred always to call Himself the "Son of Man," and as the writers of the Gospels chose the material for their work, He inspired them to choose just such details as emphasized His feeble, human side. By doing so, He knew, if again with reverence we may say it, that He was risking very much. He knew that men would use it against Him; He knew that generation after generation would take up this undeniable evidence and cast it in the teeth of His defenders. He knew that it would be for the fall as well as for the resurrection of many in Israel.[103] Yet He preferred that the risk should be run. He preferred that insult after insult should be offered Him then in the flesh, and afterward in the Spirit, rather

---

[103] See Luke 2:34.

than that men should say that He in any way fell short of His title: the "meek and humble of heart."[104]

One prophecy of Him, at least, should not be frustrated: that "He hath borne our infirmities and carried our sorrows."[105] It was from His heart that He cried, "Blessed is he that shall not be scandalized in me,"[106] yet, when His fellow townsmen "wondered and said: 'How came this man by this wisdom and miracles? Is not this the carpenter's son? Is not His mother called Mary, and His brethren James, and Joseph, and Simon, and Jude? And His sisters, are they not all with us? Whence therefore hath He these things?' And they were scandalized because of Him"[107] — when all this happened, He made no effort to undeceive them. The evidence they brought was too valuable for the end He had in view. Yes, even though He was compelled broken-heartedly to cry out on its account, "All you shall be scandalized in me this night,"[108] He was willing and preferred that so it should be.

What, then, was the end He had in view? It is not very far to seek. While He lived among men, it is true, it would be easy enough to recognize His manhood, but how would it be when He was gone? His memory would be handed down from one to another; the wonderful things that He had done would be recorded. From time to time, it might be, the tales that were told of Him would be overcolored; at any event, the distance of years and the barrier of death would separate men from any true experience of Him. How much easier would it then be to believe that He was indeed very God, but that He was man only in appearance!

[104] Matt. 11:30.
[105] Isa. 53:4.
[106] Matt. 11:6.
[107] Matt. 13:54-57.
[108] Matt. 26:31.

God had appeared on the earth before. He had walked with Adam in the garden, yet had not been man. He had appeared to Moses in the bush, yet had still been God, and not a fire. He had thundered from Mount Sinai, yet it had been no more than a manifestation. He had filled the Ark and the Temple with His presence, yet there had been no thought of any assumption of a new nature. Might it not, then, be the same on the occasion of this last manifestation? Might God-made-man be no more than God appearing as man, as He had appeared in other ways before?

He knew that this doubt might be; indeed, He knew that it would be. Since He passed from the earth, the difficulty of mankind has been to keep its balance. Either it becomes too learned in the signs of His human nature, and so fails to see that He is God, or it is overwhelmed with the proofs of His divinity, and hence doubts—in practice, at least—the evident fact that He is man. And the second, it would seem, was the danger the most dreaded. Against it He would make the most careful preparation. If men denied His Godhead, they were not of His own, and He would leave them to the mercy of the Father; but if men denied or doubted His manhood, then He knew that they were His own who had been unable to understand. And these, above all, it was essential that He should help. He must not let them doubt His relationship with them; He must not let them think He was removed from them, that He belonged wholly to another sphere, another order of creation; that their experiences were not His own; that He did not know, and understand, and feel whatever they endured; that they were called upon to carry a burden that was not also His own. At whatever risk, this must not be permitted. Neither the greatness of His teaching, nor the wonder of His miracles, nor the confession of devils, of men, of angels, and of the Father Himself, should so exalt Him as to make His children think that He was not one of their own household.

So in all the weakness of infancy He submitted to be born at Bethlehem. He could not have emptied Himself more. From the beginning He lay at the mercy of men, at the mercy of His parents, at the mercy of Herod, helpless in the shriveled hands of Simeon and Anna, and never raised a finger as a sign of His power. At Nazareth He grew into manhood no more quickly than others, with no more striking signs to show it, so that at the end men who knew Him could wonder how He came by His knowledge. When His time for action came, He submitted, like any common sinner, to the baptism of penance; this, He told John, was but a fulfillment of justice.[109] So far did He identify Himself with guilty man — "made sin," as St. Paul later uncompromisingly put it[110] — He is led into the desert to prepare; He fasts as the price of future victory; He is tempted by the Devil. How much lower can He go? Now and throughout the years after, He shows human weakness, human needs. He is hungry in the desert, at the well of Jacob; a few weeks later, He is thirsty and worn out; more than once, as the months of His short life roll on, He is in need of nourishment and rest.

Indeed, so integral a part do eating and drinking play in the life of men that He would leave no doubt upon this head. He eats with His friends, and He eats with His enemies. He eats with Pharisees, and He eats with publicans and sinners. His first formal appearance before the world is at a marriage banquet. Some of His most momentous lessons are delivered across the table; some of His most wonderful acts of condescension are performed in the midst of eating. He shows His friendship by dining with those He loves. He rewards His converts by sitting down at their table. For it He even submits to be taunted: "Behold a man that is a glutton

[109]Matt. 3:15.
[110]2 Cor. 5:21.

and a drinker of wine, a friend of publicans and sinners."[111] He is entertained by Simon the Pharisee, by Levi the publican, by Simon Peter the apostle, and by Lazarus, raised from the dead. It is at table that He institutes the Blessed Sacrament, and even after His Resurrection He eats to convince His disciples that He is not a spirit, and by others He is recognized "in the breaking of bread."[112]

But if His body was so very human, needing food and drink, needing rest and sleep, what shall we say of His quivering human soul? "Who is weak, and I am not weak?" says St. Paul. "Who is scandalized, and I am not on fire?"[113] In another place he says, "Be ye followers of me, as I am of Christ";[114] and elsewhere, "He was made in all things like to man, sin alone excepted."[115] Put the three together, and we have the truth; and our Lord has taken care that this, too, shall be stamped upon the Gospel story. When a young man comes to Him, led by a generous ideal, the Heart of Christ bubbles with affection: "Jesus, looking on him, loved him."[116]

When He meets a poor widow wailing for the loss of her only son, He is "moved with pity"[117] and cannot contain Himself. When people do not thank Him, He is hurt; when they do, He overflows with gratitude. He has a tender place for children, and no less tender a place for wistful, half-despairing sinners — for Zachaeus and Levi and Magdalene and Peter. He is roused when His friends are abused, enthusiastic when they are praised, compassionate

[111] Luke 7:34.
[112] Luke 24:30-31.
[113] 2 Cor. 11:29.
[114] 1 Cor. 11:1.
[115] See Heb. 4:15.
[116] Mark 10:21.
[117] Luke 7:13.

when they are suffering or in want, indulgent as a mother when they are being tried. And, to crown all, He breaks into tears—cries because a dear friend is dead, cries again at the thought that His own Jerusalem had failed Him.

Then there is the story of the Passion—a story of human weakness without a parallel. The Evangelists strain to find words that will adequately describe Him as He enters upon it. "He began to be sorrowful, and to be very troubled." "He began to be dumbfounded." "My soul is sorrowful, even to death."[118] These are the phrases with which they bring Him upon the scene. But that is a story by itself. Even without it, of one thing we are certain: that Jesus Christ is very man. "It behoveth Him in all things to be made like unto His brethren, that He might become a merciful and faithful High Priest before God, that He might be a propitiation for the sins of the people. For in that wherein He Himself hath suffered and been tempted, He is able to succor them also that are tempted."[119]

[118] See Matt. 26:38; John 13:21.
[119] Heb. 2:17-18.

Chapter 17

You Are Called to Heroism

Of every child who is born, the question is soon asked: What will become of him? The fond mother has her dream within her heart from the beginning, often enough regardless of the child's capabilities. The father looks on and calculates, considering time, place, and circumstances. The teacher has other ideas, usually built upon a knowledge of the nature as it develops. Soon the child himself begins to realize himself, comes to the use of reason, as we call it, reaches out toward ideals that he sees, whether they be true or mere phantoms, and longs to have them for his own. At first he scarcely knows what they are; at first he does not know his own powers. Gradually, by experience and humility, he learns both the one and the other, what is in itself attainable and what he may himself attain, and as he grows to manhood, he aspires to build up his life accordingly.

But whatever the process of training may be, in the event the making of the man depends very much upon the child himself.

"Men at some time are masters of their fate," says Shakespeare. We would like to add, not merely "at some time," but from the beginning to the end. Others may help us or thwart us; circumstances may be for us or against us. They cannot wholly make us or destroy us. We must labor at the making ourselves, and it is never wholly completed.

And in the process we may recognize with ease the divisions under which the makers of themselves may be classified. Ultimately there are three—not wholly distinct, it is true. In some things a man may belong to one type, in others to another; but, generally speaking, in the matters that count most for his making above all, in those things that count most for the making of his inner self, we shall find one or another of three characteristics prevailing, by which the whole man and his whole career are colored.

The first type may or may not be the most common. There are few in whom some trace of it may not be found. It goes by many names. In childhood, it is called self-indulgent; in youth, it is weak-kneed and wanting in backbone. The man in whom it is conspicuous is either given ugly names, or else he is pityingly condoned. It is the type that is represented by him who has an aspiration to be the best that his nature will permit him; who wishes to accomplish all that for which he has been made, but who, for one reason or another, never seems to come to anything. On one excuse or another never puts his hand to the plough, much less, having put it there, takes it back again.

At school he looks on at those who succeed better than himself. Some leave him behind in studies. He attributes it to their quicker brains, their better opportunities, their greater freedom from obstacles. Others excel him in athletics. He tells himself they are stronger built, more agile, less hampered by sickliness of body. Others, again, are more cheerful and more popular with their companions. He puts it down to their natural wit, their natural fertility of mind, some gift or another that he does not possess.

In youth he watches his equals leaving him behind. He solaces himself with the thought that he has not had their chances, that he has not been so fortunate in his results, that he does not have their almost superhuman energy, that he has been born under an unlucky star and must be content.

In manhood, when beginnings are apparently no more, he submits to the inevitable. He was not made to succeed; his lot was cast in humdrum and humble ways; he must be content to be one of the ordinary many with nothing very special about him. Perhaps even he gives himself comfort from the thought that the ordinary many, the "unknown and the valued as nothing," are greatest in the sight of God.

If this judgment of himself were really true, there would be nothing more to be answered. But no man is ordinary, if only because of the simple fact that no two men are alike. And as for the honor of being "unknown and valued as nothing," let it be remembered that it is those who "strive to be unknown" — not those who lie down under their burden — that receive the reward of the just. A man may not, indeed, be what is called clever; he may not be fleet of foot or agile; he may not have the readiness of wit to utter a *bon mot*, or to make some brilliant repartee. But none of these excuses him from sitting down idle and listless; none justifies his being contented with inaction at any period of his life, drifting aimlessly like a ship without a rudder, a gossamer at the mercy of every breath of wind, a poor boneless creature that cannot stand up straight, because it has had neither energy nor courage to make itself. It has always told itself that it wished and looked and hoped for better things; it has known it could do better if it chose. All it has said have been only excuses, and not reasons. An uncanny nagging spirit has forever haunted its undeserved, endless hours of resting. Jogged by this spirit, it has persistently intended to start afresh; but the day of starting has always been tomorrow, and tomorrow has never become today.

The second type is much more common, particularly, perhaps, in this generation, when getting on is so much the fashion. It is the type of those who do more than merely wish and then idly stand still. They determine to succeed, but their success must be in their own particular way. Whether or not it is actually the best way matters little. Whether success is to be gained at the sacrifice of others is secondary. Such things must happen, and in these days, every man must look to himself. Whether even for the man himself it is best, it is futile, he holds it, to inquire. Somehow or other, he must get on; that is the matter of first importance. Some particular way of getting on has taken his fancy; to pause now and reconsider is to lose precious time.

In a child, this tendency of mind is an unlovely thing. We blame it as self-seeking, if not worse. Even in those who are grown up, when it is too flagrant, when it settles down to mere self-preferment, to mere money-making and the like, we may, indeed, envy, but we feel ourselves justified in at least affecting to condemn. But when it is not too manifest, we condone it; we even give it honorable names.

There is too much fellow-feeling between it and ourselves for our judgment upon it to be too rigorous. We more than half-encourage it in children; in youth we call it worthy ambition; in a man, if only he succeeds, we crown it with honor. No wonder so many take it as their rule of action, for it is the rule that is sanctioned by the whole world's estimate of life. Right or wrong, a man must get what he wants; that is his business here. If he were to fail, he might be more a man. That is not to the point. Were he to succeed along some other course, more fruitful, perhaps, but less according to his inclination, he might deserve better of his fellowmen. He cannot now afford to chop and change. Success in his own present course may entail misfortune to others, much ultimate regret to himself. The first is not his affair, and as for the second, let the future look after itself.

Such is the second type of men, the characteristic type of our present generation, whether or not it is the most common. It is a type that can harden the human heart into steel. Nothing can make a man so hard as the worship of success. It is true it brings with it a certain sense of satisfaction—that is, if only it succeeds. But if it fails! And everyone does not succeed. The greater number fail altogether. Probably none reach the final goal of their ambitions. But even if they partially succeed, the result is very different from that which they expected. There is always disappointment mingled with the victory. There is always the little more that might have made all the difference; always the disillusionment that comes with every triumph; always the sense that, after all, if they had chosen another road, they might have gone much farther. Such a man may accept the situation and say that he is content; but his contentment demands an act of the will. It is not the spontaneous result of a nature satisfied.

And there is a third type, which is the type of a very man. It is the type that is guided by the desire to do the right thing, whatever the right thing may be. To a man of this type, getting on is not the all-in-all; it is not even everything to keep what belongs to himself. He knows that in the world there are other men besides him, other interests besides his own. He knows that right and wrong are not subjective matters only; that he may not define them just as they suit his convenience; that others, too, have rights, and others have wrongs, and theirs may have the greater claim. He knows that, in the long run, right can never interfere with itself, and wrong will prove its own condemnation; that one man's self-seeking is no sanction for the same in another; that if he fails in consequence, because of the unequal contest, he does a nobler thing, is a nobler man, and lives a nobler life than if he succeeded by any less worthy tactics. He knows that he honors the man who goes down in such a struggle more than his unscrupulous rival who succeeds; that failure, not success, is both the making and the proof of the hero, whether in the end it is rewarded or not—failure by death on the field of battle, failure by death in an Antarctic blizzard, failure by death on a leper island, failure by martyrdom, or in any other way, when standing for truth against injustice. These are the things even this world knows how to honor; therefore, the man in whom they are most alive is a man in the fullest sense.

It is true the type is not common. Not every man is a hero, whatever he might be or might once have been. Time saps enthusiasm. Winners of the Victoria Cross are more often young than old. Indulgence saps the power to give and the power to make an effort. It becomes easier to submit and justify our submission than to stand up and be shot "for nothing." But here, at least, in whatever else it must yield place, youth has the advantage over age. It can make itself be, and it can make itself do, what more matured years cannot; and when a man stands up for the right, and takes the consequences, we know what a man can be.

Of the first and second type we have no more to add. Whatever they are, however comfortable, however prosperous, the honor we pay them cannot be more than lip service. But the third is an ideal and makes us look. It makes us wish many things for ourselves, whether we can aspire to it or not. But can we not? That is, indeed, the whole question.

We may think it is too much for us. We may fancy we have lost our opportunity. We may say our day for such making is past. We may reckon up our failures and ask whether, with such a record, success can ever be hoped for. In a hundred ways we may plead to be dismissed and suffered to remain second- or third-rate. But human nature pleads against itself. It answers that the power that has made can also unmake; that the creature which has voluntarily accepted the yoke can also set itself free. It is true we cannot all be heroes, if by heroism is meant something that depends upon accidental guts, something that must shine conspicuously before the eyes of other men. But if it means a constant aspiration for the right; if it means a steady march toward it, no matter what may tempt us to look elsewhere; if it means an unflinching refusal to be beaten, however often the enemy may have us down; if it means a strong determination that the right thing shall be done in us and by us, at whatever cost to ourselves—then yes, even we can be heroes, even we can never be conquered, and not to be conquered is to win.

Chapter 18

You Are Called to Give God Your Very Self

If in the natural order it is true that men in the making fall under three types, more or less, equally is it true in the supernatural. The spiritual side of man has its counterpart in the material. The natural virtues are not wholly distinct from the supernatural; they need only readjustment for grace to make them the same. The whole man is neither the one nor the other but is both combined. Christ our Lord came not to destroy, but to perfect. Grace does not eliminate human nature, but takes what it finds, and lifts it up, and the methods of growth along both planes are parallel. The man of no natural spirit will never make a saint; neither will the man who, with all his spirit, nevertheless seeks his own ends, however seemingly good those ends may be. It is only the hero, even judged by natural standards, who will do supernatural deeds of heroism.

This at first may sound a hard saying, but is heroism easy, and is sanctity different from any other kind of heroism? If it were, there would be many more saints, as St. Teresa very clearly told her followers. But whether it is hard or not is beside our present purpose. We would rather examine the parallel that exists between the supernatural life and the natural; how the three types seen in the one are no less seen in the other. Of these, the first includes a large number—perhaps the greatest number of all. It may not at once be easily distinguished.

At the outset, the spiritual life is often smooth enough and offers little opportunity for seeing differences. We begin with our first notions of what is good and right. With these first notions, human nature easily concurs, for, in spite of all that is said against it, human nature in itself is good and tends toward goodness. When supernaturalized, it still remains complacent, so long as it is left alone. But grace has a way of being troublesome. It never leaves a soul quite satisfied with itself or with the smooth and easy path it is treading. It is forever asking for more. It is not content with an oblation that costs the giver nothing. It tells the soul that receives it that the only gift to God worth giving is the gift that He Himself desires—that is the only gift worthy of a man. When that is realized, then comes the rub; then we can begin to see to which type a soul makes up its mind to belong.

Or, rather, we should say that the first type is of those who never make up their minds at all. There is a calling of grace in their hearts, but its words convey no meaning to their minds. They hear it, as it were, at a distance, but they make no effort to draw nearer. They may suspect its message, but they cannot be quite sure, and they prefer to remain in doubt. If they listened more carefully, they might know, but they suspect that the knowledge might, just here and just now, be inconvenient.

Of course, they do not utterly wish to reject the call; they would not be accused of throwing God's grace away. Someday they mean to be better men; someday they will set about it in good earnest. Even now, if they knew what precisely had to be done, they would try to do it. But for the present, they do not know; for the present, they have other things on hand, and they can only act according to their lights. So they argue with themselves, with their backs turned to the light, seeing darkness where in reality is only their own shadow. So the morning of life expands into the noontide, and the laborer stands idle; the noon draws on to evening, and he tells himself that now it is too late. He will try again tomorrow, but the tomorrow on which he will begin never, never dawns.

There is a second type of spiritual-mindedness, the one that makes most show of being in earnest, but also the one that is most apt to proclaim its disappointment and failure. The man belonging to this type has grasped quite well the meaning, and the fascination, and the glory, and the fruitfulness of the supernatural life. He has recognized the greatness of the saints, the whole new world opened up by the insight of prayer, the invincible strength that is developed by personal independence and self-renunciation, the successfulness of failure, the joy of suffering, the might of littleness, and all the other paradoxes which are "to the Jews a stumbling block, and to the Gentiles foolishness, but unto them that are called, both Jews and Greeks, Christ the power of God and the wisdom of God."[120] He has recognized all this, and he has determined that he will be a member of this camp. He will take hold of the spiritual, of the supernatural. He will bring it into his life. He will adapt his life to this perspective. He will advance in spiritual experience, in prayer, in mortification, in good works, in self-sacrifice, and in knowledge and love of God. Indeed, he has long since done so. Already he has made many an effort. He has a worthy list of sacrifices to show, a worthy record of battles that he has fought. If he cannot boast of many glorious victories, of many elevations in prayer, or of many consolations in his work, he rests

---

[120] 1 Cor. 1:23-24.

on the assurance of spiritual writers who tell him that this may in itself be a mark of divine approval.

But there is one exception in it all. A man of this caliber is exposed to one great danger, and few indeed are those who escape it. It pursues everyone who aspires to the spiritual end; it pursues everyone to the end. Not only does it hide itself successfully, but it pleads with a pathos that can scarcely be resisted that it is no danger, that it is human nature's rightful rest. One who can determine what he will do can also determine what he will not. He can make up his mind what he will win, but he can also settle with himself what shall be the price beyond which he will not go. He can reason pros and cons, profits and losses, advantages and their opposites. And he can tell himself, without using any words, almost without letting himself know that he is hinting it, that there are certain things, there is at least one certain thing, he cannot forgo, no matter what may be the prize at stake. Some things, he says, are now part of himself, or at least part of the oneness of his life. To part with them would not be generosity; it would be foolish, almost suicidal, perhaps even tempting God. In any case, God cannot be so hard as to demand this snperhuman sacrifice. Other things he can bring himself to surrender; he can even give God an equivalent in kind. This one thing he cannot. It is too trifling; it is too much his own. The Power that asks for it asks for more than human nature is capable of giving. So he goes on, affecting to be convinced that he is justified, unaffectedly refusing to admit the possibility of error. He does not argue the matter; it is safer to assume that there can be no other side. Against this one tiny atom that he retains for himself he puts the many things, the great things he has given, and is still ready to give; and he satisfies himself that if everything is not wholly on his side, at all events the balance is overwhelmingly in his favor.

So he goes on from beginning to end. In most cases he will not be distinguishable from others. He will make progress in his way; he will be a "good" man "according to his lights," as the phrase goes. If he fails in this point or that, it will be put down to the weakness of human nature. In all this, he will be like his fellowmen. Even the saints must be given some kind of margin; and whether or not he responds to the one grace that matters, who can tell? None but his own soul can answer that; and even his soul, if he is persistent and determined, can be put to silence. If he will refuse to hear, there will come at last a time when hearing is scarcely possible. In noise and confusion, or with muffling and deadening of sound, the cry may be cut off altogether. Such is the second type—the type of failures, great and small. It has many grades, from great sinners who will do all but give up their dominating passion, to those on the verge of sanctity who fail because of some trifling bondage to step across the border. But for all alike, whether they be sinners or potential saints, it is unworthy.

The third type alone is noble. It is no less ambitious than its predecessor; indeed, it is more. It has made up its mind no less; it has done more. But it differs from the other in this: it must put no limit to the price that may be demanded. It has no secret possession of its own; no heirloom or treasure with which it will not part. It has lost itself and its own claims in the vast otherness of this world and the next; or, rather, it has lost itself, and this world besides, in the vast otherness of the next.

"Aeterna non caduca,"[121] said one little hero fired with this understanding. "Quid hoc ad aeternitatem?"[122] said another; and life, according to that motto, produced heroism of the very highest

---

[121] "Forever not doomed to die."
[122] "What is this to eternity?"

grade. Such a life does not merely keep back anything for itself; it forgets that there is anything to keep, or that there is a self to serve. Man loves and honors selflessness. There is no selflessness to match that which has drowned itself in eternity.

Chapter 19

Prayer Is the Raising of Heart and Mind to God

It is striking to notice what a fascination the very mention of the word *prayer* has for every type of human being. Describe a man as a man of prayer, and you mark him as something exceptional, something to be revered. Mean what you say when you so describe him, and you do him the greatest honor that one man can do to another. A man of prayer is understood to be a man apart. He is assumed to possess a learning, and sources of learning, that the best of universities cannot give him. He sees visions and dreams dreams that the deepest of poets cannot fathom. When he speaks, his words are full of wisdom. When he chooses to act, he is known to be guided by an understanding, an insight, a deliberation, a maturity of judgment that make his deed ineffably fruitful. The man of prayer is the power in the world that tells, the summit of human perfection that is at once our pride and our desire; perhaps also sometimes our despair.

Or again, let a book on prayer be written, and it is astonishing how great will be the number of its readers. Let it become known that it really does teach something of profit, and its immortality is well-nigh guaranteed. From all this and much more besides, the fascination of prayer is manifest. There can be little doubt that human nature longs to pray, that it longs to know how to pray, that to learn how to pray is one of the cravings of every human being.

And yet the disappointment of it all! For how many does the desire to pray aright end in something very like despair! At first it seems an easy and sweet thing. The books seem to make it natural and progressive, a straight high road, with hedges and ditches on each side and innumerable signs to point the way. The lives of the saints, and even the lives of some around us who are not yet saints, seem to show us prayer as a realized fact, a habitual atmosphere, and not a mere succession of experiments. And we are led, indeed we are almost compelled, to conclude that it should be the same with us, that if we ourselves were better men or if we were better instructed, and that if we fail, it is due either to ourselves and our lack of effort, or to our ignorance of the science. We try to remedy the evil, and the evil always remains; if we seem to succeed in removing it for a time, it still forever returns. We hunt about eagerly for hints and suggestions, and the hints we get come to nothing. We try new books, we listen to new teachers, we adopt new methods, we alter our subject matter, and the result is always the same. We go around and around in a circle; our prayer makes no progress. On the contrary, it becomes a weariness; the old interests drop off, the old attractions grow stale, the old order changes, and there is no new order to take its place, and we fall to the ground dizzy and distracted by the unceasing round upon round of the same monotonous routine.

This is surely not as it should be. What is more, it does not appear to have been always the same. Ancient spiritual writers tell us much about prayer, they explain and combat many other difficulties in its way; but the particular kind of despair that is now so common is almost unknown to them. It seems to belong to our own generation, our own peculiar understanding of life;

and, indeed, this is probably true. Probably we should find, if we examined closely, that in this, as in other matters, the meaning of the word has changed; that our definition of prayer differs not a little from the definition accepted by our forefathers; that we look for that in prayer which they never dreamed of seeking; and that much of our disappointment is due, not to the prayer itself, nor to any want of progress on our part, but to the simple fact that we fail to find in it that which, if we were wise, we would never try to find.

The first and greatest hindrance to prayer is sufficiently obvious when examined. It arises in part from the spirit of the age in which we live; but partly, too, from the practice of a thing in itself very good. This is an introspective, self-analyzing generation. Our novels are full of it; our conversation teems with it; our poetry is almost nothing else. We tear our poor hearts to tatters to see how they are made. When our hearts wince beneath our probing fingers, we call ourselves martyrs; when they cease to beat altogether we grow melancholy, disappointed, and morbid. So is it, or so is there danger of it being, in the spiritual life as well. At first, when we begin to pray there is all the joy of unreflecting childhood in its practice; we leap forward generously to the light, and run, with dilated hearts, in the way of God's commandments.

But presently we are warned to be cautious; we must not go too quickly; in a sense we must not be too expansive, for fear we will make a fatal mistake. The warning is only too welcome to a nature such as ours. Immediately we begin to stop short and analyze. We become two persons in our prayer, one of whom watches the other; while we try to pray, we also try to study ourselves praying. We analyze our motives, our methods, and our results. Some fruit that God in His goodness has given us in prayer we think to gain again by some device of our own. We are no longer little children skipping in the sunshine; we become the nurse who watches lest they fall; or rather, we try to be both nurse and child in one, and so end in being neither. We lose that spontaneity, that simplicity, that self-annihilation in prayer without which progress and relish are impossible. We prevent the bulb from growing by constantly examining its roots; by picking at every bud, we destroy all hope of blossom or fruit.

This is not the method of the saints, not of any one of them. There is much more in prayer than mere examination of conscience, more than the mere framing of a resolution, very much more than self-analysis, self-gratification, or the study of our relation with this life. The very definition of prayer, framed by theologians and saints, accepted by the Church, and taught to her children, young and old, does not include any of these. Prayer is, as the catechism tells us, "the raising of the mind and heart to God" — "*elevatio mentis ad Deum,*" as St. Thomas defines it. Self-examination and resolution may be included in it; they are in no way its essential parts. I may examine myself that my prayer may be made better. I may discuss the prayer itself so that faults may be avoided in the future. Resolutions may be the outcome of my prayer, the reaction, as it were, upon this life after one has had some insight into the other. But above and before all else, it is the raising of the mind and heart to God that matters, and my prayer is then best when I do this most effectually, leaving earth alone, leaving myself alone, realizing God and even a very little of that which He means, and letting my tiny soul prattle to the Lord in whatever feeble way it may, once it has come in contact with Him. This is of the essence of prayer; without it prayer is not. The most perfect examination of conscience, the most pointed of resolutions, if made for their own sakes, or based on rational motives, and without raising mind and heart to God, may not be rightly called prayer.

On the other hand, prayer is possible without either examination or resolve; although underneath it all, it is difficult to see how prayer that is deep will not, implicitly at least, contain both the one and the other. He who raises mind and heart to God cannot help but be and become a better man; and to become a better man must involve somewhere both self-examination and determination.

It follows from all this that prayer has many forms and many grades. There is no one "method" that satisfies all souls or even the same soul at all times. The Jesuit Father was himself an experienced man of prayer who regularly advised his clients, "Pray the way you like best." Indeed, this is the one way to learn, the one way to make progress. Prayer is not a philosophy; it is not an abstract science; it cannot be learned from books; it cannot be taught by theory.

To know about prayer and to be a man of prayer are by no means always the same thing. Prayer is a life, an activity, and to make progress in it, we need to practice it as we know it. This alone keeps prayer true; and prayer that is not true is futile vanity, if not worse. This alone keeps prayer real, part of ourselves; and prayer that is not that is sheer imitation.

Let us learn to take our poor little souls as we find them. Some of us, a very few, may possibly begin high; the majority of us, who are nonetheless "called to be saints," will find perfection on a lower gradient. But whether high or low, our best will be according to our powers and only by using the powers we actually possess can we learn to do more. For some, prayer will be the constant repetition of a word or a phrase or a form; for others, the concentration on a single thought or idea; for others, again, who aspire to meditation, a sequence of thoughts leading from one definite point to another; but all—be it never forgotten—raising the mind and heart to God. If I do that, I succeed in prayer, from whatever starting point I set out, in whatever way I proceed, and at whatever goal I arrive.

Chapter 20

You Influence Others by Your Example

It is a truism to say that the influence we have upon each other by our mere contact with one another is well-nigh infinite. So true is it that modern philosophers are found to build upon it an entirely new theory of life. They see in it so great an interference with free will as to render it entirely negligible. They deem our lives so inextricably intertwined that we must all of necessity be judged, and stand or fall, together. Darwinism, Altruism, Eugenism: what are they all but subtle applications of this theory? Even Pantheism, Hegelianism, and their latest progeny, Modernism, are all fashioned of the same material. This, at least, they have in common with one another, and in common with universal truth; whether we like it or not, we are, to a very great extent, the victims of our surroundings, and especially of those with whom we come in contact.

In our ordinary life, this is emphasized at every turn. It is true that underneath, away below the waters that the gale can stir, there is the independent "I," which can, and must, make itself. Nevertheless, the character of the man, the color of his mind and heart and soul, the prejudices and the sympathies, the limitations and the possibilities, the greatnesses and the littlenesses, the ideas and opinions he adopts and defends, even the religious beliefs and the spiritual impressions that he has made his own, depend much more than he is always willing to allow on circumstances outside himself—circumstance of birth, circumstance of education, most of all, perhaps, the apparently chance circumstance of some individual having crossed his path.

In the case of others, we see it very plainly, even if we do not always see it very plainly in ourselves. If we have any care at all for our children, we are solicitous as to the companions with whom their lives are cast. We pick and choose their instructors so far as we are able. We keep a watch on the making of their friendships. We are restless when we find them going their own way. We know very well that to leave them entirely to themselves to develop as they may is an act of cowardice on our part, an act of infidelity to them. It is in vain for us to shirk this responsibility. We may say that our children must go through the fire like the rest; that they must not be brought up in a hothouse; that in the end, greater experience means greater strength. When the end does come, and the son has become the victim of evil habits, the daughter has shaken off all parental control, we may learn how much of the misfortune is to be laid at our own door. The fallacy of modern education—every one of us sees it—is not that of curriculum, of subjects to be taught, or of the qualification of those who are to teach them. It is to suppose that teaching and learning will make a good man, will save him from evil influences, and will compensate for any lack of care on the part of those who should be his protectors. "Let our children, let our poor, be taught, and they will become good citizens." Never was a fallacy more patent, more belied by facts, and yet more blindly accepted as the cure of the evils of men.

And there is the other side, the countertruth to all this. If we are ourselves much more the product of our surroundings than we always realize, if others enter into our lives and affect us for time and for eternity, much more deeply than they can imagine, no less true is it that we in our turn have our effect upon others. No man can so shut himself in as to be able to make his own world without consideration of his fellowmen. We owe as much as we receive. We may resent it; we may cry with Cain, "Am I my brother's keeper?"[123] We may close our eyes to our surroundings; we may shut ourselves up in our castles and defend ourselves with moat and drawbridge. The fact will still remain that a man cannot be a good man without making other men better. A man cannot be bad without other men being the worse for it.

Indeed, we sometimes ask ourselves whether this is not one of the reasons God is so angry with sin. If He so loved the world as to give His only Son for its redemption, what must He not think of him whose influence has tended to undo His work? "It were better for him that a millstone were tied about his neck, and that he were cast into the depths of the sea"[124] is the wording of the curse pronounced on those who scandalized the little ones of Christ, quite regardless of the offense committed against God Himself; and it helps us to understand why He declared the Second Commandment, "Thou shalt love thy neighbor," to be like unto the First, "Thou shalt love the Lord thy God."

There is no need to work this point. We know how far it leads. When we reckon up the worth of our lives, how often do we measure them by the influence for good or for evil that they may have had upon those around us? How often do we find even the conscious sinner plead in his defense that "he has done no harm to others"? Nay, more, much as a man may demand to be left alone,

[123] Gen. 4:9.
[124] Mark 9:41.

much as he may resent the tax that is made on his moral nature for the benefit of his fellowmen, there is nothing in another he will more contemn than this deliberate shirking of duty. "Am I my brother's keeper?" is an appeal that betrays a hardened heart, against which a brother's blood cries out to Heaven for vengeance.

But it is not for such that these words are written. They are written for those to whom the good of others is an interest and a care; who, even in the moments when their own pending doom will not keep them from evildoing, yet will be deterred by the thought of the injury they may do to others. They have themselves been so defended in the past—often enough to their knowledge, still more often when they have not known it; now comes the occasion for them to give freely what they have freely received.

And not only that. There is something more in this truth that should be no small consolation and encouragement to anyone who will think of it: the consoling certainty of the untold good we may do without even being aware that we are doing it. Example is not a conscious thing; it does not submit to weight and measure; it works its effect on whoever will touch the hem of its garment as it passes by. The more conscious, the more reflex it is, the less is its influence; the more natural, the more spontaneous, the more unconscious, whether in its nature or in its actions, so much the more is it part of the man in whom it lives, and therefore is the more far-reaching. Hence, it is far removed from mere formalism, still more from anything that savors of hypocrisy. It has nothing to conceal; it has no secret ends to gain. It just is what it is, and does right because it is, and gives because it cannot keep it. So spontaneous, so single-minded, is true example; and when it is that, it produces its effect, even when faults are many.

The angel who watches over good example is very sensitive and shy. He will not have us look aside to see what effect we are producing. He resents our peeping over his shoulder to see what good deeds he records. He shuns and disdains the least self-congratulation that prides itself even a very little on the model to others that it affords. He would have us go straight on, looking neither to the left nor to the right, except it be to warn ourselves of the vast responsibility of merely being, and of the vast consequences for good or evil that may attend every good or evil step that we take.

When I think of myself alone, evildoing is a shameful thing. When I think of God, it is accursed. When I think of others, it is criminal.

Chapter 21

Christ Calls You to Suffer
with Him and with Others

It needs a saint to understand the Passion, let alone to enter into it. The rest of us can do little more than stand by the roadside and look on. We are among the crowd while the grim procession passes by; we are seldom part of the procession. Sometimes, it is true, we follow after, "a long way off"; we have a haunting desire "to see the end,"[125] but we wait until the shouters have dispersed, and there is little or no fear of our being taken for "one of them."[126] We are interested sometimes; sometimes, when the picture is beautifully painted, or the story is vividly told, we are moved and even affected. We feel sympathy; perhaps we have tears in our eyes and a choking in our throats, but usually this is the farthest we can reach. The gathering breaks up, and we make our way home, to our dinner, to our newspaper, to our next amusement, to our daily routine and occupation. We are much the same after as before.

[125] See Matt. 26:58.
[126] Matt. 26:73.

Overcoming Worldly Concerns

I do not say this in blame; I only say it is the matter of fact. The most appalling event in history can leave us thus unchanged, in spite of our declared faith and love.

It is true we do not lose everything. Onlookers in the crowd gain something from the Passion, if it is only a soul-scorching memory; but only a saint, who walks side by side with the Master, who shares the stripes and the insults and the Cross, and knows the Man who is its center figure, can have any real understanding of all that the Passion means.

He alone can read the nature of that Heart whose every fiber was made for suffering—sensitive to right and wrong, to good and evil, to harmony and discord, as that of the finest artist; meek and enduring, because it felt in itself every strain on the heart of another; spotlessly sinless, and therefore all the more appalled and sickened at the sight of sin; master in the school of suffering, because, from its very nature, it drew to itself every suffering of every human soul.

He alone can grasp the depth of that ocean of suffering in which the Victim was engulfed—foreshadowed from the beginning in successive type and prophecy, in Abel and Isaac, and the paschal lamb, in Moses and David and Isaiah and Jeremiah and John the Baptist; foreshadowed and emphasized in every step of His career, from Bethlehem and Egypt and the Temple, through the long years of prayer and loneliness and silent waiting, the days when men handled Him roughly, and "would not."[127] Over all His life, over all the lives of the people who prepared for Him the way, even we can watch the dark cloud gathering. What, then, must not a saint discover!

Only a saint, again, can put himself completely in the place of Christ, can suffer alongside or in His place, can be truly and perfectly sympathetic and compassionate, so that his own fevered

[127]Matt. 23:37.

heart, and every quivering nerve in his body, responds to, reproduces, the throbbing of pain in the body of the Master. Such was the suffering of Mary on Calvary. To have been nailed upon the Cross that stood up before her—how great would have been her relief! Such was the compassion of St. Catherine of Siena, of St. Mary Magdalen of Pazzi,[128] and of many more of their kind, whose power of compassion has stamped the marks of the Passion on their bodies. Such was that of St. Francis of Assisi, of St. Francis Xavier, of St. Philip Neri, of St. Thérèse,[129] whose hearts must needs burst their natural bounds since the Heart of Christ had been broken. And such is the secret of countless hidden saints, in this generation when hidden saints are many, who are in agony, they know not why, and it is because they cannot suffer along with Him as they would; or who find joy in the midst of sorrow, again they know not why, and it is because their soul then most responds to the soul of the Man of Sorrows.

We need not look far afield for confirmation of this truth. We have experience of it in ourselves. We see it in our friends. We know it in every pang of life that lifts us upon its wave. The suffering of others affects us in different degrees, according to the nearness of those who suffer. A stranger may merely interest; an acquaintance will at least win a word of compassion; a connection will stir us to relieve; one we love will rouse our whole being, will

---

[128] St. Catherine of Siena (1347-1380), Dominican tertiary; St. Mary Magdalen of Pazzi (1566-1607), Carmelite nun who patiently bore grievous trials of body and spirit.

[129] St. Francis of Assisi (1182-1226), founder of the Franciscan Order; St. Francis Xavier (1506-1552), Jesuit missionary to the East Indies; St. Philip Neri (1515-1595), Italian priest who founded of the Congregation of the Oratory; St. Therese of Lisieux (1873-1897), Carmelite nun.

drive us frantic, will make our sympathetic pain even greater than that which gives it. A child is dying in great suffering, but what is the suffering of the child compared with that of the mother, who merely sits and looks on? A son or daughter is disgraced, but what is his or her shame to that of the father whose good name has now for the first time been tarnished?

So great an agony is true compassion. Given perfect love, we know the suffering that it will entail; but only those who know the one have known the other. The time may even come when they will know what it is for human nature to be crushed beneath the weight of its own cross of sympathy. By the suffering of one it loves, human nature is first drawn and then is repelled; first it revels in companionship, and then breaks down and would flee. In the extreme of sympathetic sorrow, by the bedside of one who is very dear to us, or in the company of one who has been cruelly wronged, there comes a moment when we seem unable to endure any more, when our gorge seems to rise against the very pain itself, when a sense of sickness comes upon us, when the strong man must stand up, and pace about, speechless, aimless, apparently torn with rage, while the woman sits still, lifeless, staring into space, incapable of any attention, with a weird look of wrinkled age upon her features.

"At the Cross her station keeping / stood the mournful Mother weeping / close to Jesus to the last." Have we ever in our lives gone through anything like this? If we have, let us thank God for it. It is a possession for all time. It is an experience that has brought us one stage nearer to Calvary. Now we know a little better what the compassion of the saints must be. In this lies their secret; this explains why suffering had for them so great a fascination, why they "delighted that they were accounted worthy to suffer,"[130] why one

---

[130] Acts 5:41.

saint cries, "Either to suffer or to die!" and another, "Not to die, but to suffer!" Their delight was to them no narcotic; if they joyed in suffering, they suffered nonetheless on that account. None were greater sufferers than they, even though none were more happy. But as to every man that has a heart, suffering of our own is a right and a privilege when we stand beside a friend who suffers, so, and much more, do the saints claim suffering as their right, and rejoice when their claim is heard, because of their suffering Lord, with whom they are in love.

So it is that the Cross of Christ has transformed the world of suffering. "I, when I shall be lifted up, will draw all things to myself";[131] He has drawn to Himself, and has nailed to His Cross along with Himself, all the suffering of all mankind. It has given suffering a new meaning, given it a new significance, actually made it the greatest delight on earth to those who completely understand. To those who do not, and to us insofar as we do not, suffering is still a problem and an evil. To the Jews, Christ crucified is still a stumbling block, and to the Gentiles, He is still foolishness. But "to them that are called" He "is the power of God and the wisdom of God"; and even a little of this wisdom is a treasure beyond all price.

Still it must be remembered that this joy is the fruit of the Cross; it is not the Cross itself. Happy though we may be in carrying it, carry it nevertheless we must. The happiness will not heal the galling wound, nor lighten the weary feet, nor lift the load of depression. Often, perhaps always, for us the light goes out in the midst of suffering; it is only before it begins, or after it is over, that we see the good thing it is. Nor, we may reverently think, was it different with our Lord. Before His Passion He "had a baptism wherewith

---

[131] John 12:32.

He had to be baptized,"[132] and He could not be restrained from hurrying toward it. When it was over, He could glory in it all and rejoice that it had been necessary. But during it, we are expressly told, He was "sorrowful even unto death"; He was "amazed and depressed"; He prayed that the chalice might pass from Him; He cried out with a loud voice, "My God, my God, why hast Thou forsaken me?"[133]

In this, more than in anything else in the Passion, earnest souls come near to Him in sympathy; here, more than anywhere else, might they, if they would, find joy "that they are accounted worthy to suffer something" for His sake. Yet how strangely they fail to recognize the fact. Likeness to Christ our Lord in His depression is no less a proof of His love than is any other likeness that He condescends to give; it may be that it is the greatest proof of all.

---

[132] Mark 10:38.
[133] Matt. 27:46.

Chapter 22

Mary Exemplifies the Greatness
to Which You Are Called

"And the virgin's name was Mary.[134] There can be no doubt that this name meant something in particular to the author of the third Gospel. Notice how he dwells upon it; notice how he breaks his former sentence to give it a sentence by itself; notice how in its own sentence it holds by far the most emphatic place. It is not so with Joseph's name. That comes in its natural order: "A man, whose name was Joseph," and it would have been more natural for St. Luke to say, "A virgin, whose name was Mary," especially as she is mentioned before her spouse. Yet no; he has mentioned her first, but her name he keeps to the end.

We are fond of great names. By means of names we write our history and help our memories. Often enough, sometimes without warrant, a simple name will stir all our enthusiasm. The merest mention of her child's name is enough to make many a fond mother's heart beat more quickly. When friends are separated, the name and no more suffices to keep each other's memories alive.

[134] Luke 1:27.

And in general it may be said the more men and women really are to one another, the more real is their affection for each other, so much the more are their names cherished by one another, as if in them were contained everything they wished to remember. They need the name and nothing more to recall in all its fullness one another's recollection.

What, then, should the name of Mary mean to us, as Catholics, as Catholics who are proud to belong to her dowry, to claim her special friendship, and more? It sums up all she is to us, and all we are to her. It contains all that is meant by devotion; that is devotedness—to her, and in our hearts we know what that implies. The name of Mary brings her up before us, her figure, her features, her expression. We recognize her, her placid countenance, her quiet eyes, her lips around which the shadow of a smile forever lingers, her unruffled brow, her whole demeanor under control, as if we had time and again met her face-to-face. The name of Mary tells us all she has been and is to us; and the recollection fills us full of gratitude and fire.

The name of Mary reminds us of what we are to her, and surely there is nothing that gives us a stronger sense of hope. "Sweet is thy name, O Mary, to the poor exile's heart," says the hymn, and it is true of each one of us, no matter who we may be—strong men who are not given much to sentiment, or weak women, who are sated with its excess; great sinners, whose consciousness of guilt, or whose reckless use of life, has all but stifled all they had of affection, or innocent souls, still open to deep feeling; rich or poor, young or old—for all of us, the name of Mary is one that makes us raise our eyes. "At the name of Jesus every knee shall bow";[135] at the name of Mary, every head shall be lifted up.

[135] Phil. 2:10.

Have we ever, in our prayers or at other times, tried to picture to ourselves what kind of a woman our Lady must have been? If she were living in our world today, in our own generation, in our own streets among us, where would we be most likely to meet her? And if we did meet with her, what kind of woman would we find her to be? Would we come across her in hallowed surroundings, seated apart, as the Italian artists painted her, or in some way marked as royal, as she was portrayed by the early Greek Christians?

We often think and speak of virtue as if in this wicked world it were a thing impossible. It cannot be expected, we assume, that men and women in ordinary surroundings should be holy above the common. Holiness, if it is to be preserved and fostered, must be put away, in some convent, or monastery, or institute that will shield it from the contamination of the world. And so, perhaps, we suppose it would have been with our Lady. Were she living now, we would expect to find her in some convent, possibly in some hospital, but not in the humdrum, weary, toiling world in which we live.

What is more, wherever we might find her, we feel sure we would recognize her sanctity. Such holiness, we tell ourselves, could never be hidden. It would be seen in her face; it would betray itself in her every action. We assume it is so in a saint; how much more in the Queen of saints! There would be something in her manner, something in her speech, something in her great devotion and piety that would set her apart from all others and would compel us to say, as soon as we saw her, that now we had found her and could not be mistaken.

It is possible we may be right. If our Lady were living now, she might, indeed, have been found in some convent cell, and we might have been able to distinguish her from others by reason of her special holiness. Still, if we are to judge from the picture given of her by the Gospels, it does not seem very likely. The Mary who is there described is no especially secluded soul; she is just a village maiden, and no more. She is not set apart in some particularly holy place; the village where she lived was on one of the high roads of the country. She came into the world, not at an especially holy time, nor among an especially holy people; the Jews of her day were not what they had been. They had passed through trouble and oppression and sin, and had been singed and scarred in the process. Nor, again, when we find her in her home at Nazareth, do we find a maiden marked among her companions for holiness, or held in veneration by the women of the place. She is described as just "a virgin espoused to a man whose name was Joseph,"[136] and no more; the only other thing the Evangelist has to say is that "the virgin's name was Mary," and on that, as we have said, he seems to linger.

Indeed, so much is she like any other woman of her village that at a late time, when our Lord made His appeal to His own people, it was cast in his teeth that He came of so ordinary a mother, and that therefore He could not be the Prophet or Messiah. " 'Is not this the carpenter,' they said, 'the Son of Mary?' And they were scandalized in regard of Him."[137]

Sometimes it is our good fortune to come across, and get to know, some simple and quiet soul whose only possession seems to be its innocence, whom all the world passes by as being too ordinary and of no account. Does not such a soul have some resemblance to our Lady? Sometimes we have met a child of Adam, always contented with his lot, whether one of joy or one of sorrow, whether full or empty, always faithful to his duty, whether easy or difficult,

[136] Luke 1:27.
[137] Mark 6:3.

always at peace with those around him, patiently seeking not his own, looking for no return, and for the most part receiving none, taken for granted by his companions and therefore for the most part ignored. May not such a soul be like our Lady? Sometimes we have seen inside a heart, perhaps of a mother, perhaps of a friend, who has seemed to others cold and colorless, reserved and of little feeling, but to us has shown itself overflowing with scalding love and affection. Is such a heart very unlike that of our Lady?

Mary, the simple maid of Nazareth, yet declared "Blessed among women"; Mary, the outcast Mother of an outcast child, and yet the very Mother of God; Mary, the silent wonderer, who spoke but little and passed through life little noticed, who "understood not" all her Son said and did, but kept it and pondered it in her heart,[138] while the rest of men forgot it; Mary, the secluded onlooker, while her Son went out to save mankind; Mary, the faithful companion, who stood there while her Son was hanged before her; Mary, triumphant now in Heaven, but with her Mother's nature unchanged: this is the Mary of the Gospels, the Mary whom we know, the Mary whom God and men delight to honor. Never have men been more dearly shown that notoriety is not greatness. Nowhere does hiddenness more clearly appear as identical with heroism. In no other case is sanctity, perfection, seen more emphatically to consist in truth of life whose very evenness is its concealment.

[138] Luke 2:49.

About the Author

Alban Goodier, SJ (1869-1939), was a Jesuit who served for a time as archbishop of Bombay, India. He was renowned for his memorable aphorisms: "A friend is the one who comes in when the whole world has gone out"; "the enthusiastic, to those who are not, are always something of a trial"; and many more. He was also a well-respected writer who contributed many articles to the magazine *The Messenger of the Sacred Heart*. He wrote over a dozen books, including *Saints for Sinners*, *The Passion and Death of Our Lord Jesus Christ*, *The Inner Life of the Catholic*, and *The School of Love*.

Sophia Institute

Sophia Institute is a nonprofit institution that seeks to nurture the spiritual, moral, and cultural life of souls and to spread the gospel of Christ in conformity with the authentic teachings of the Roman Catholic Church.

Sophia Institute Press fulfills this mission by offering translations, reprints, and new publications that afford readers a rich source of the enduring wisdom of mankind.

Sophia Institute also operates the popular online resource CatholicExchange.com. *Catholic Exchange* provides world news from a Catholic perspective as well as daily devotionals and articles that will help readers to grow in holiness and live a life consistent with the teachings of the Church.

In 2013, Sophia Institute launched Sophia Institute for Teachers to renew and rebuild Catholic culture through service to Catholic education. With the goal of nurturing the spiritual, moral, and cultural life of souls, and an abiding respect for the role and work of teachers, we strive to provide materials and programs that are at once enlightening to the mind and ennobling to the heart; faithful and complete, as well as useful and practical.

Sophia Institute gratefully recognizes the Solidarity Association for preserving and encouraging the growth of our apostolate over the course of many years. Without their generous and timely support, this book would not be in your hands.

www.SophiaInstitute.com
www.CatholicExchange.com
www.SophiaInstituteforTeachers.org

Sophia Institute Press is a registered trademark of Sophia Institute.
Sophia Institute is a tax-exempt institution as defined by the
Internal Revenue Code, Section 501(c)(3). Tax ID 22-2548708.